PORTFOLIO/PENGUIN

LIKE A VIRGIN

Richard Branson is the founder of Virgin Group. He was born in 1950 and educated at Stowe School, where he set up *Student* magazine when he was sixteen years old. In 1970 he founded Virgin as a mail order record retailer and shortly afterward opened a record shop on London's Oxford Street. Two years later the company built a recording studio and Virgin Records went on to become one of the top six record companies in the world.

Since then, Virgin Group has expanded to encompass more than four hundred companies in over thirty countries. Branson is the only person in the world to have built eight billion-dollar companies from scratch in eight different sectors. Through the Virgin Group's charitable arm, Unite, he is working to develop new approaches to social and environmental problems.

Branson's autobiography, *Losing My Virginity*, and his books on business, *Business Stripped Bare*, *Screw Business As Usual*, and *Screw It, Let's Do It*, are all international bestsellers. He lives on Necker Island in the British Virgin Islands and is married with two grown-up children.

RICHARD BRANSON

Like A Virgin

Secrets They Won't Teach You at Business School

PORTFOLIO/PENGUIN

PORTFOLIO/PENGUIN

Published by the Penguin Group
Penguin Group (USA) Inc., 375 Hudson Street, New York, New York 10014, U.S.A.
Penguin Group (Canada), 90 Eglinton Avenue East, Suite 700, Toronto, Ontario, Canada
M4P 2Y3 (a division of Pearson Penguin Canada Inc.)
Penguin Books Ltd, 80 Strand, London WC2R 0RL, England
Penguin Ireland, 25 St Stephen's Green, Dublin 2, Ireland (a division of Penguin Books Ltd)
Penguin Group (Australia), 250 Camberwell Road, Camberwell, Victoria 3124, Australia (a
division of Pearson Australia Group Pty Ltd)
Penguin Books India Pvt Ltd, 11 Community Centre, Panchsheel Park, New Delhi – 110 017,
India
Penguin Group (NZ), 67 Apollo Drive, Rosedale, Auckland 0632, New Zealand (a division
of Pearson New Zealand Ltd)
Penguin Books (South Africa) (Pty) Ltd, 24 Sturdee Avenue, Rosebank, Johannesburg 2196,
South Africa

Penguin Books Ltd, Registered Offices:
80 Strand, London WC2R 0RL, England

First published in the United Kingdom by Virgin Books, an imprint of Ebury Publishing 2012
First published in the United States of America by Portfolio/Penguin, a member of Penguin
Group (USA) Inc. 2012

10   9

Copyright © Richard Branson, 2012
All rights reserved

ISBN 978-1-59184-568-3

Printed in the United States of America

Contents

Foreword

Business schools are wonderful places and yet, in hindsight, I am thankful I never went to one – assuming that is that any of them would have had me!

The simple fact is that formal education and I were never really meant for each other. I suffered from an acute combination of dyslexia and what I suppose would nowadays be diagnosed as attention deficit disorder. When I went to Stowe School in the sixties however, I was simply regarded as an inattentive and troublesome student. As a result I think everyone from the headmaster down was probably rather relieved when I decided to drop out and pursue my dream (at that time) of publishing my own magazine.

Had I pursued my education long enough to learn all the conventional dos and don'ts of starting a business I often wonder how different my life and career might have been.

Although the word was allegedly first coined in the nineteenth century, I certainly had no idea when I started my magazine and subsequent mail-order record businesses that I was also displaying some quite marked symptoms of something called 'entrepreneurship'.

I

While the word would have meant nothing to me then, it has since become pretty much the core of everything I have done for the last forty-plus years. The Virgin group of companies has grown in some weird and wonderful ways that even I don't always quite understand. Sometimes I wonder if the fact I was never indoctrinated into the 'correct' way of doing something is why, come what may, I seldom have trouble sleeping at night.

I talk a lot in the articles I hope you are about to read about the important role I believe entrepreneurs have to play in this world. The creative juices that lead to entrepreneurs starting and reviving businesses not only create employment but also help tackle some of the many challenges facing our communities, society and the planet.

Entrepreneurs are innately curious people. This must be why I receive loads of mail from people all around the world asking all manner of questions on doing business 'Like a Virgin'. The following pages are a blend of responses to questions I have received, as well as an assortment of my written ramblings that have appeared in various publications around the world.

The people who contact me tend to be looking for advice on everything from starting a new business to closing an old one, from hiring people to firing them and – the fun part – everything else in between. Given my well-known focus on business always being enjoyable and fun, the boundary between my work and my personal life does sometimes tend to blur a little: so too do the questions I receive!

As I have never worked for anyone, this book is written through the eyes of a founder. However, the advice is pertinent for anyone faced with the challenges of working in a business or company.

Just recently in London a British interviewer asked me a great many short questions about both my work and my personal life; so by way of introduction to what's to follow, these were some of the more interesting exchanges:

Q: What's the first thing you think of when you wake up?
A: *Like most people, I think about the time! Often followed by 'What country am I in?'*

Q: Which single word gets you out of bed in the morning?
A: *It's three actually, 'Richard. Stop that!' in my wife's Glaswegian accent.*

Q: Which is your favourite band?
A: *Okay, I'm biased but it has to be the Sex Pistols and Mike Oldfield, who were both the genesis of Virgin Records – oh yes and Genesis, too.*

Q: Which was the first record you bought?
A: *I'm embarrassed to say, I think it was Cliff Richard's 'Summer Holiday'.*

Q: Best country you have visited?
A: *Tough call, but probably Australia. I just love the Aussies' zest for life – a wonderful, vibrant country.*

Q: Favourite country?
A: *Much as I adore living in the British Virgin Islands it has to be the UK. It's been very kind to me over the years.*

3

Q: Three most adventurous things you have done so far?

A: *Trans-Atlantic speedboating, hot-air ballooning and kite surfing. Space adventure is still to come although, ironically, it may be the least dangerous thing on this list.*

Q: If you could meet a legend, dead or alive, who would it be?

A: *I assume you'd bring them back to life for the meeting? If so either Christopher Columbus who, among a lot of other places, first sighted the British Virgin Islands, or Sir Francis Drake. I'd love to have been an explorer of that calibre.*

Q: Who is your mentor?

A: *My mum and dad. They've both been a tremendously positive influence on my life.*

Q: What is the greatest piece of wisdom you've ever heard?

A: *To look for only the best in people. And if I can have a second one, 'Only a fool never changes his mind.'*

Q: Favourite song?

A: *Frank Sinatra's 'My Way'. Probably not the coolest answer you'd expect, eh? Especially from someone who once owned the biggest independent record label in the world.*

Q: Has anyone ever mistaken you for somebody else?

A: *Quite often. Once, a little girl came up to me and said, 'You look just like that Richard Branson bloke.' And I nodded and said thank you. She then said, 'You should go and sign up for one of those lookalike agencies. You might not make as much money as him, but you would still make a fortune!' I also get Brad Pitt all the time ... just kidding!*

Q: If you were given $60 to start a business, how would you do it?

A: *If I were well known, I'd sign the dollars and sell each of them for $20. I would then sign the $20 and sell them for $50 and so on. As they say, nothing makes money like money!*

Q: Is there anything you'd like to change about yourself?

A: *It'd have to be my age. I'd like to start going backwards instead of forwards.*

Q: What do you love and hate?

A: *I love the closeness of our family. And I hate not being able to spend a lot more time with them. Actually, I also hate the word 'hate'. There's way too much of it in this world.*

Q: What makes you cry?

A: *I cry at happy and sad things. My kids always bring a box of Kleenex to the movies! I've also seen a lot of sights in places like Africa that would bring tears to anyone's eyes.*

Q: What makes you laugh?

A: *I'm lucky. I laugh all the time. I love life, I love people, love a good joke. I really subscribe to the theory that laughter is good for the soul.*

Q: What's contributed most to your success?

A: *All the people who've worked their tails off at Virgin over the years and have made it what it is today. There's been some luck mixed in, for sure, but I believe luck doesn't just happen – you have to work at it.*

Q: The key to success in three words, please?
A: *People. People. People.*

Q: Anything you still want?
A: *I'd like some grandchildren, as would my wife. Fingers crossed!*

Q: What motivates you to carry on?
A: *Everything! I love what I do, I love people, love making a difference. I don't think I'll stop until I drop. Why would I? I'm having too much fun.*

Q: What drives you crazy?
A: *Negativity. People who only look for the worst in others and 'glass half-empty' types. I can't stand gossips!*

Q: Are you stressed?
A: *Not really. I try hard to overcome challenges and, if I fail, I pick myself up quickly.*

Q: What keeps you awake at night?
A: *It used to be partying but that's a rarity these days. Now, very little keeps me awake at night. I usually sleep like a baby.*

Q: What is your biggest fear?
A: *Like a lot of people, I fear illness in our family or friends. Things I cannot control.*

Q: Are you ticklish?
A: *I'm the most ticklish person I know. Although just why it is that you can't tickle yourself remains one of life's greatest unsolved mysteries.*

Q: What brings you happiness?

A: *Achieving things that one can be proud of, especially when people said it couldn't be done.*

Q: Which one of the seven dwarves would you be?

A: *Is there one called Horny? No? Okay then I suppose I'd opt for Happy!*

Q: Has there been an event that changed your life?

A: *Surviving the hot-air balloon and speedboat crashes, which meant I was around to meet Nelson Mandela. He's an utterly incredible man; I'm truly privileged to know him.*

Q: Ever thought about running for political office?

A: *No. I don't think you can mix business and politics. I'd have to give up Virgin and I enjoy it too much. I can campaign for (and against) a lot of political issues without actually becoming a politician.*

Q: What is the most embarrassing thing you've ever done?

A: *Well, the one I'm prepared to talk about was probably one time when Ruby Wax and I were in Mallorca. A young couple came up to us and asked something about taking a photo. So Ruby and I put our arms round each other, smiled, and the couple looked confused and said, 'No, we want you to take a picture of us.'*

Q: Who would play you in a movie of your life?

A: *I used to answer that question with 'me' but was never sure I'd be handsome enough for the role. Just kidding! Probably Robert Pattinson from* Twilight. *He's British and he's young!*

Q: If you were not you, who would you want to be and why?
A: *I'd love to start again, and be my (still to get here) grandchild when he or she is born.*

Q: Anybody of whom you are still in awe?
A: *That has to be the Archbishop Tutu.*

Q: What is your favourite sport?
A: *I love skiing, and I play a lot of tennis, but right now I'd have to say kite surfing. It's unusual, I know, but we've got the best conditions for it on Necker.*

Q: Did running the London Marathon hurt you as much as it did me?
A: *I don't know how much it hurt you, but yes! The last few miles were pretty tough going, but the crowd was amazing and their enthusiasm carried everybody along. I highly recommend it.*

Q: Three words to describe the Virgin brand?
A: *Innovative, fun and quality-service-at-a-great-price. I cheated a bit on that last word!*

Q: Anything left for you to achieve?
A: *One of the most exciting things we're involved in is the Elders. Trying to ensure that world conflicts are resolved more effectively or even become a thing of the past. I believe we are going to see the Elders achieve some fantastic things.*

Q: Is there anything you'd have done differently?
A: *With the gift of hindsight of course there are a lot of things I should have done differently, but in its absence the answer is no. I've had an absolute blast and hope to keep doing so for a long time to come.*

FIVE SECRETS TO STARTING A BUSINESS

And making it work

There are two questions I get asked all the time. The most popular is 'How did you come to name the business Virgin?' A close second is 'What's your secret to successfully building businesses?'

The first is easy to answer but the second one always takes some thinking about. The fact is that there's no one thing that characterises Virgin's many successful ventures or, for that matter, what went wrong when we didn't get it right. Reflecting across forty years, however, I have come up with five secrets for improving the chances of a new business surviving and with luck – something we all need – flourishing.

I. If you don't enjoy it don't do it

Starting a business takes huge amounts of hard work and time so you had better enjoy doing it. When I started Virgin from a basement in west London, there was no great plan or strategy. I didn't set out to build a business empire. I simply wanted to create something people would enjoy using, have fun doing it and at the end of the day prayed that it would make enough to pay the bills.

For me, building a business is all about doing something to be proud of, bringing talented people together and creating something that's going to make a real difference to other people's lives.

Business people are not unlike artists. What you have when you start a company is a blank canvas; you have to fill it. Just as a good artist has to get every single detail right on that canvas, a businessman or woman has to get every single little thing right when first setting up in business in order to succeed. However, unlike a work of art, the business is never finished. It constantly evolves and it's also not that easy to paint over your mistakes!

If a businessperson sets out to make a real difference and achieves that objective, he or she will be able to pay the bills and have a successful business to boot.

2. Be innovative – create something different

Whether you have a product, a service or a brand, it is not easy to start a company and to survive and thrive in the modern world. In fact, you've got to do something radically different to make your mark today.

Look at the most successful businesses of the past twenty years. Microsoft, Google, Apple and Facebook all shook up the world we live in by doing things that had never been done before and then by continually innovating. They are now among the dominant forces.

Not everyone can aspire to such levels; however, should you decide to enter an already crowded segment you had better be ready to offer customer service that blows the competition away.

When we started Virgin Atlantic the positive buzz that we created focused on the simple fact that our crews were really nice to our passengers. Go figure – what a breakthrough idea for an airline!

3. Pride of association works wonders

Businesses are nothing more than a group of people, and they are by far and away your biggest assets. In fact in probably the majority of businesses your people *are* your product.

For me there is nothing sadder than hearing someone being apologetic about the place where they are working. When people are proud to be associated with their company it generates a special level of advocacy and dedication that is a huge differentiator in a world full of mediocrity and indifference.

4. Lead by listening

To be a good leader you have to be a great listener. Sure, you need to know your own mind, but there is no point in imposing your views on others without some debate and a degree of consensus. No one has a monopoly on good ideas or good advice.

Get out there, listen to people, draw people out and learn from them. As a leader you've also got to be extremely good at lavishing praise. Never openly criticise people; never lose your temper, and always be quick to applaud a job well done.

People flourish on praise. Usually they don't need to be told when they've done wrong because most of the time they know it.

5. Be visible

A good leader doesn't get stuck behind a desk. I've never worked in an office – I've always worked from home – but I am constantly out and about, meeting people. It seems I am travelling all the time but I always have a notebook handy to jot down questions, concerns or good ideas.

If I'm on any of the Virgin airlines I always try hard to meet as many of the cabin crew and passengers as possible, and will usually come away with a dozen or more good suggestions or ideas. If I didn't write them down I might remember only a few, but putting them in the infamous notebook means I remember them all. Talk to your staff and customers at every opportunity, listen to what they tell you, good and bad, and act on it.

Some might say, 'Well, all that's easy when you have a small business', but at Virgin we strive to appoint company heads who have the same philosophy. That way we can run a large group of companies in the same way a small business owner runs a family business – keeping it proactive, responsive and friendly.

Oh yes: I still have to answer that first question as to the origin of the Virgin name. Sadly there's no great sexy story to it as it was thought up on the fly. One night, I was chatting with a group of sixteen year old girls over a few drinks about a name for the record store. A bunch of ideas were bounced around, then, as we were all new to business, someone suggested Virgin. It smacked of new and fresh and at the time the word was still slightly risqué, so, thinking it would be an attention-grabber, we went with it.

But no matter how good the concept and/or brand name, even the best of them can fail at the first attempt. For example, in the early sixties, another group with a catchy name, the Beatles, were turned away by no fewer than seven record labels before they found one willing to take them on.

So, if you don't survive, just remember that the majority of new businesses don't make it and that some of the best lessons are usually learned from failure. And like the old song says, 'Just pick yourself up, dust yourself off and start all over again'.

PEOPLE POWER

The real engine of any business

Let's get right to the point: good people are not just crucial to a business, they are the business!

Finding them, managing them, inspiring them and then holding on to them is one of the most important challenges a business leader faces, and your success or lack thereof plays a vital role in the long-term success and growth of your business.

What is a company but a collection of people? Take an airline – the aircraft it flies are pretty much the same as its rival's. The interiors are usually much of a muchness and there is often only a slight difference in the entertainment and food. What sets one airline apart from its peers is its people (aka cabin crew) and their attitude towards their passengers. Our Virgin airline crews are smiling, cheerful and pleased to help, which leaves our passengers wanting to fly with us again.

It is no surprise that, like Virgin Atlantic before it, Virgin America, which flies within the United States, constantly sweeps the travel awards for service and quality. Its planes are new, with great interiors and entertainment; but above all, the great service of its crews is what wins so many plaudits.

People are your key asset. On the front lines of business, they can make or break a company. As I constantly remind our managers and other budding entrepreneurs, a true sense of pride in the business makes all the difference.

Even the best people need great leadership. A good leader must know the team, its strengths and weaknesses; socialising and listening to the team face to face is key. One of the most common reasons people leave a job is because they were not listened to. It's rarely just about money, more often about frustration.

Like the proverbial bad apple, a bad leader can destroy a business very quickly. In small businesses this is easily apparent. On my island of Necker in the Caribbean, we once had a new general manager who tried to change the way things were done. Among other things he discouraged the staff from socialising over an occasional drink (or two!) with our guests, which rapidly soured the island's historically collegial atmosphere. We had to step in to replace the manager and restore staff morale and the sense of management's trust in them, which had been broken.

We also started some of our most successful businesses after pitches from our people. Virgin Blue, for instance, our Australian airline, (now known as Virgin Australia) was the brainchild of Brett

Godfrey, an Aussie who had been working for Virgin in Brussels.

As only an Australian could, he came to me with his business plan written on a beer mat – outlining the start-up of a low-cost domestic carrier in Australia to take on Qantas and Ansett. In the intervening decade Brett has expanded Virgin Australia and its sister airlines to the United States, New Zealand, Thailand and Bali.

In other cases, we backed an outside team when we were sufficiently impressed by them to give them brand support and the space to go and build the new business themselves. Virgin Active, our health club chain, is a good example. Matthew Bucknall and Frank Reed came to me with the idea of a family-friendly health and fitness club in 1999. They had set up and sold a chain in the United Kingdom in the 1990s and wanted to do it again with the Virgin brand on the door.

We liked the idea and the management team, so we backed the rollout in the UK, and within two years were offered the opportunity (by Nelson Mandela himself!) to rescue a chain in South Africa. The Active team jumped at the chance and haven't looked back since. We now have more than one hundred clubs in South Africa and another hundred and sixty in the UK, Australia, Italy, Spain and Portugal.

Trust is a key facet of any business, but how you deal with being let down once can also contribute to success. Are you willing to give people a second chance?

When I was running Virgin Records, a member of the talent-scouting team was stealing and selling boxes of records to local secondhand shops. Tipped off, I called him on it. He admitted everything. Rather than fire him, I gave him a severe warning and a second chance. Everyone messes up sometimes, I told him, and I said I expected him to learn from his mistake and get back to doing what he did best – finding artists. He went on to discover Culture Club, one of our biggest-selling artists of the 1980s.

We all slip up at some stage in our careers. I did. When I was just a teenager, I fell foul of British customs as I was trying to sneak duty-free records out of the UK. I escaped a criminal record by paying a fine and was given a second chance. I think this has made me much more accepting and forgiving of other people's mistakes.

So many companies compare themselves to family units that the word 'family' appears to be sorely overused in modern business. However, I really believe that Virgin's family spirit has kept it flourishing for over forty years.

When the business was smaller, we had legendary parties at my house near Oxford. We set up a fairground with tents full of entertainment for the staff and their families. As we grew, the party turned into two parties and, pretty soon, they were two-week parties with 80,000 people just to make sure everyone was invited. By the end they had become three-week parties, and at that point the neighbours cried, 'Enough!' (and my hands cried 'enough') and we had to stop.

But we had established the culture – one built around people. People are the lifeblood of any company and, whether the neighbours like it or not, they need to be looked after and celebrated again and again!

NICE GUYS CAN FINISH FIRST

Teaming beats steaming

Perhaps I give the impression of being a 'nice guy' but, one way or another, one philosophical question I am frequently asked is whether or not nice guys can finish anywhere but last in the dog-eat-dog world of business.

The question usually goes something like this: 'I have been trying to get my business off the ground, and I often feel that I have to get very aggressive with suppliers and service providers. I hate being aggressive, but have come to believe that only very aggressive people get ahead. I hate it more when my success (and survival) is hampered by others who don't perform as they should. How have you handled this in Virgin?'

Let's consider the issue of aggression. There are lots of ways to get your point across and make your business successful without being aggressive. Always remember that you love what you do and your role is to persuade others to love your business, too, and, therefore, to want to work with you.

I like to think that we are successful at Virgin because we engage with everyone in a positive, inclusive manner rather than in an aggressive, combative or negative way

If the companies or individuals you deal with do not respond to a positive approach, ask yourself if they are the companies you should work with. For every supplier out there that is aggressive, there are another five that will want to work with you – in a way that allows you and your business to be true to a more inclusive and positive partnership.

I agree that a strong personality is a great asset when starting up or running a business, but 'strong' doesn't have to equate to 'aggressive'. The key skills are confidence in your ability to follow your vision, the ability to listen to others and the art of delegation.

It's often hard to get past your own feelings of frustration when dealing with others. Delegating to a member of your team brings a fresh pair of eyes and ears and often a different approach and perspective.

One of my key lessons over the years has been to surround myself with great management teams who complement me and ensure that we have the all-round skills to make our businesses succeed. Our chief executives at Virgin Group and businesses like Virgin Active, America, Atlantic, Trains and Money have built strong businesses blending their personalities and skills on top of the Virgin culture I helped found.

As for negotiation: the key is to remain calm and collected. If you are getting angry, take a deep breath, realise you are taking it too personally and take a step back. Rely on those around you to help you out. Teamwork will usually carry the day. .

You can negotiate competitively without aggression. Understand what you want to achieve and what leverage you possess to help you reach your goals. Less aggression and more determination is what you need.

I often find, after a tough set of talks, that it is good to go out for a drink and get it off your chest! You may have a sore head in the morning but relying on and confiding in your team will often help you put everything in a clearer perspective.

Entrepreneurs have to make tough calls. Does this require a ruthless streak? I don't think I'm ruthless (although a few people who have never met me have portrayed me that way!). Actually, it is counterproductive to be ruthless. People tend to come back and do more business if they feel they have done well with you. Over the years this attitude has helped me to attract and keep good partners and staff.

My willingness to listen to other people and accept it when their suggestions are better than mine has served me well during my forty years in business. I'm never too proud to admit I'm wrong or take action when others' suggestions are better.

Remember to have fun. There is no point in being in business if it is not fun. Have fun with your team, your suppliers and the companies you work with. It is so much more rewarding to build up a healthy rapport than to find yourself in a constant battle. Don't take everything so personally. Let your hair down now and again.

And as to who finishes first or last, does it really matter? I for one would far rather be a nice guy working with great people having fun with a small successful business than a miserable guy heading up a hugely profitable multinational mega-corp.

But that's your call.

THE WEAKEST LINK

Great customer service is a chain

I have always liked Sam Cooke's old hit song 'Chain Gang'. It really comes in handy when I'm talking about customer service.

That's because delivering good customer service requires that a front-line worker receives supportive assistance from an entire network of co-workers – in effect, a chain reaction of teamwork, one that is consistent from beginning to end. And when it comes to helping a customer, the chain of assistance is only as strong as its weakest link.

I love hearing reports of good care, especially when they're shared by a Virgin customer. But no matter what the source, there's usually a lesson to be learned.

Just to prove that I'm not always bashing our favourite competitor, British Airways, I'll tell a (true) consummate customer story that involves that other British airline.

An Executive Club passenger sitting aboard a jumbo jet about to leave London for New York suddenly realised he'd left his beloved leather coat in the airport lounge. He rushed to the front of the plane and asked if he had time to get it. 'Sorry, sir, too late,' replied a member of the cabin crew. 'But don't worry. I'll tell the ground crew and they'll have it sent to you.' He returned to his seat, convinced he'd never see his favourite coat again.

Seven and a half hours later, when the flight arrived at JFK International Airport, the passenger was amazed when an agent met him at the door of the aircraft and handed him his coat. They'd put it on a Concorde flight that had beaten his slower 747 across the Atlantic!

(Of course, I am obliged to point out that British Airways can no longer pull off that particular trick as, sadly, the speedy Concorde is now a museum piece. However, there is hope that Virgin Galactic may fill that void one day.)

It's true that the airline could have put the coat on a later flight and the customer would have been just as grateful when it arrived. But going the extra mile builds massive customer loyalty and brand-enhancing benefits. You can be sure that passenger talked up the airline for years, and now even the founder of a rival company is telling the tale. How great is that?

Let's look at another story that clearly demonstrates the importance of every link in the service chain – this time involving Virgin Atlantic. An Upper Class customer's free limo failed to connect with him at his New York City hotel. (It turned out the customer had been waiting at the wrong door.) He jumped in a cab to Newark Airport, a fair distance from the city.

Rush-hour traffic was bad; by the time he got to the airport he was very angry, running late, and panicking that he'd miss his flight.

The first Virgin agent he located immediately seized control of the situation. She calmed the fuming customer, apologising profusely, and assured him that he would not miss his flight. From her own pocket, she refunded the taxi fare he had paid, then she rushed the passenger through a staff lane and got him to the gate with ten minutes to spare.

Truly a job well done! Like the leather jacket incident, it demonstrates how great customer service can convert a negative into a positive.

Now we come to the part of the story where the chain breaks. During the post-flight debriefing, the agent told her supervisor what had happened and asked to be repaid the $70 cab fare she had dispensed. Rather than congratulating the agent on saving the day, the supervisor asked whether she'd got a receipt for the fare. When her answer was, 'Well, no, there was no time for that', the irate supervisor castigated her with, 'No receipt, no reimbursement. You'd better take more care next time.'

Clearly, the misguided supervisor was more concerned about rigid adherence to accounting practices than about employee initiative. While fiscal accountability is important, especially when an outlay of cash is involved, there will always be occasions when an asterisk needs to be marked on the balance sheet.

One thing is certain: any Virgin employees witnessing their supervisor's scornful reaction to their colleague's exemplary deed would be unlikely to display the same resourcefulness. Which means that the customer loses – and so does the entire company.

Happily, the story came to the airport manager's attention and he quickly took steps to redress the imbalance between company procedure and customer service. He advised accounting that he'd approved the cash shortfall, while the supervisor got a quick refresher on how important it is to 'catch people doing something right'.

I heard this story eventually, and it truly impressed me. The next time I flew through Newark, I made a point of seeking out the agent who had made us proud. I remarked, 'I don't have a taxi receipt, so you probably can't help me.' Her astonished smile said it all.

No company can train its front-end people to handle every situation, but you can strive to create an environment in which they feel at ease 'doing as they would be done by'.

Good customer service on the shop floor begins at the very top. If your senior people don't get it, even the strongest links further down the line can become compromised.

Finally, poor customer service can also be relished ... if you experience it at the hands of a competitor! At such moments you might catch me humming another old favourite, Aretha Franklin's 'Chain of Fools'.

BUSINESS PHILOSOPHY
Five quick questions

I thought it would be helpful to answer a few more of the interesting questions I am asked on my travels.

I. What is the best advice you ever got?

Three gems come to mind. First, an enduring one from my mother, Eve, who always taught me never to look back in regret but to move on to the next thing. The amount of time people waste dwelling on failures rather than putting that energy into another project always amazes me. My mother also told me not to openly criticise other people. If she heard me speaking ill of someone, she would make me stand in front of the mirror for five minutes and stare at myself. Her reasoning? All my critical talk was a poor reflection on my own character.

In the 1980s Sir Freddie Laker, the British airline tycoon, gave me a great piece of advice on setting up my own airline. He told me two key things: 'You'll never have the advertising power to outmarket British Airways. You are going to have to get out there and sell yourself. Make a fool of yourself, whatever it takes. Otherwise you won't survive.' He also wisely said: 'Make sure you appear on the front page and not the back pages.' I've followed that advice ever since. I've been very visible and made a fool of myself on more than a couple of occasions!

2. And the worst advice?

I'd never embarrass the person who gave it by revealing that, but they know who they are! Look, advice comes in many forms. I believe in never asking just one person but in getting as much feedback as possible. Opinions always vary. By asking several people what they think, you get many angles and can weigh them all. This way, you are never considering just one person's opinion, so no one piece of advice is ever truly bad.

3. What advice would you give to young entrepreneurs on how best to start?

To remember that it is impossible to run a business without taking risks. Virgin would not be the company it is today if we had not taken risks along the way. You really do have to believe in what you are doing. Devote yourself to it 100 per cent and be prepared to take a few hits along the way. If you go into something expecting it to fail, nine times out of ten it will.

Above all, remember to have fun with it. That keeps you and your colleagues enthusiastic and motivated. One of my favourite sayings (which happens, I believe, to be one of my own!) sums this up: 'The brave may not live forever – but the cautious do not live at all!'

4. In your career you've had lots of successes, but you have failed in some businesses. What have you learned from those?

One of the first times I strapped on a pair of skis the instructor told me, 'If you're not prepared to fall a lot you'll never learn to be a very good skier.' As an entrepreneur the same rule applies. You have to learn very quickly that there's no such thing as a total failure.

Looking back on Virgin's history, our ability to adapt quickly to changes has helped mitigate reverses. You must be quick to accept that something is not going well and either change tack or close the business. We run our companies lean and small with very little red tape and certainly no bureaucracy. Using our mantra 'Screw it, let's do it' we invariably make and implement decisions quickly – usually before our competitors have held their fifth meeting on the same issue.

Though I believe in taking risks, I also firmly believe in 'protecting the downside'. This means working out in advance all the things that could go wrong and making sure you have all those eventualities covered. We have come close to failure many times and most true entrepreneurs skirt close to it. We almost failed when Virgin was in its infancy and again in the early 1980s. Similarly I have nearly killed myself more than once while failing to achieve world records for boating or ballooning. But through a combination of luck and planning, both Virgin and I are still here.

5. Do you have any regrets?

There are always things in life that you might regret, and there are probably a lot of business decisions I regret – but I try not to dwell on them. I move on to more positive things.

The one missed opportunity that does rankle still was our failure to land the rights to operate the United Kingdom's national lottery. Our proposal was to run a not-for-profit game, with 100 per cent of the money going to good causes. Although we were granted the licence, the incumbent Camelot cleverly resorted to the courts to delay the process and the Commission handed the keys back to them, rather than face the prospect of no lottery at all for the few weeks it would have taken the courts to sort it out.

We have since moved on and set up Virgin Unite, our foundation, to act as a catalyst to helping others and to galvanise our companies into action. Unite has been crucial in helping us establish the Elders and the Carbon War Room, initiatives aimed at solving conflict and helping to combat climate change.

And, finally, I am often asked: are you a man of habits?

Well, yes, there are a few, but I am certainly not going to put them in writing. I guess, however, being a serial entrepreneur could be described as a pretty big habit!

SCREW YOU, GOLIATH!

Fighting the big boys

For every entrepreneurial David who has the courage to take on a Goliath with the equivalent of a slingshot and a couple of stones, there are a hundred others who'll say, 'You must be kidding! There's no way I can ever compete with that monster!'

For much of my business career, I've played the role of David – and loved every minute of it. You see, I've always believed that small is beautiful. Young, energetic businesses have surprising advantages when taking on large, cumbersome competitors. All they have to do is figure out what the giant's weaknesses are and how best to leverage them.

For instance, in 1984, when an upstart Virgin Atlantic Airways first picked a fight with mighty British Airways, the odds were certainly stacked against us. In fact, my bankers were so unenthusiastic about my prospects that they threatened to pull the rug from under us!

But our inexpensive arsenal was loaded with some pretty surprising and highly unconventional weapons. Perhaps the most effective of these was our agility, which was integral to our corporate culture, in large part because of our small size. British Airways was weighed down by bulky, hierarchical decision-making processes that made any course corrections very difficult, whereas we were able to change direction or stop on a dime.

Sir Freddie Laker once told me, 'Richard, never forget that only a fool never changes his mind.' Not wanting to be foolish, I took his good advice. At Virgin, when our customers or crew told us they didn't like something, we'd drop it and quickly move on to the next idea.

Our smallness – we had only a few planes – allowed us to give our customers an experience the bigger players simply couldn't afford to match across their large fleets. For instance, our Upper Class passengers (billed as business class; but first class in everything but name) are provided with free door-to-door limousine services to and from the airport. Our competitors would have to offer this service on every global route, not just the few routes competing with Virgin – a much more expensive proposition for them.

And consider this: if we provide limos for our business class customers, what should our competitors do for their first class customers – send them a Rolls-Royce? It didn't take them long to decide not to try to match our limo service, and almost thirty years later it remains a unique selling point for Virgin.

This may seem like a peculiar boast for a chief executive, but I don't believe a Virgin company has ever become the biggest player in any sector we have entered (although Active is getting close).

In the late eighties, Virgin Records was certainly the industry's biggest independent label, but we were far from being the biggest label overall. I kept splitting the company into smaller companies, ensuring that we kept our sense of competition and urgency.

It seemed to work. We were influential enough to attract big names like the Rolling Stones, who knew that with Virgin they'd never be just another superband on a roster full of them. At the same time, we were still small enough to be totally tuned in at street level and highly adept at discovering exciting new artists.

Now that I think of it, the one area where we probably are the biggest player is in commercial space travel. Virgin Galactic doesn't quite fit the pattern, though. Our choice to go 'To infinity and beyond!' as Buzz Lightyear of *Toy Story* would say, is more about being sufficiently courageous, visionary or perhaps plain crazy enough to establish a brand-new business sector. In fact, that attitude just about sums up our brand name.

While I believe that small is beautiful, I'm not implying that there aren't any very good companies that are very big. If you look closely, however, some of the best of them, like Apple, got where they are by focusing on great products, being nimble and competing with much bigger competitors. What Steve Jobs achieved with Apple's amazing success has brought tremendous growth – these days, those battles to survive seem a distant memory. Apple, like Virgin, must now fight to retain all the cultural elements that will keep it as nimble as its competitors and not morph into one of the ponderous giants it managed to overcome.

Now, where did I leave my slingshot?

THE IMPORTANCE OF NOT BEING EARNEST

Fun is a serious business tool

The four Ps – people, product, price and promotion – are often cited as the keys to a successful business. Yet this list omits a vital ingredient that has characterised Virgin companies throughout our forty years: Fun, with a capital F!

When we started Virgin Atlantic in 1984, we had some great people and lots of good ideas about how to do things differently. Sadly, we did not have a lot of money to take it to the streets. Compared to the giant establishment players of the time – TWA, Pan Am and British Airways – we had a tiny fleet, if one plane qualifies as a fleet, and a minuscule advertising budget. The author Anthony Sampson, pointed out that with only one plane 'we'd either have the best or worst safety record in the world.'

We could not do much about the single plane – leased from a very trusting man at Boeing. We had to make the most of our meagre marketing money. At the urging of Sir Freddie Laker, who made an art form of grabbing the limelight for his airline, I quickly became a willing victim in all kinds of wild and crazy adventures to promote the fledgling Virgin Atlantic. You couldn't buy a quarter-page ad on the front of the *New York Times*, but when my sinking speedboat or crashing hot-air balloon just happened to feature the distinctive Virgin logo, there we were!

We also started to run some funny, pretty direct and usually highly topical advertisements to grab the public's attention – I believe it's called 'jugular marketing'. Such in your face ads were largely unknown in the stodgy world of airlines, so our approach quickly gained us notoriety, press coverage and, above all, visibility. The humour stood out against our moribund competitors, and soon Virgin Atlantic itself – not just the ads – became synonymous with a cheeky and upstart personality and, more importantly, a fresh, different approach to commercial aviation.

Marketing teams in London and New York frequently reacted instantly to the day's headline news and, within twenty-four hours, placed tactical-response advertisements in key markets. The day after John Sununu, then White House chief of staff, was castigated for using public money for a limousine to take him on personal trips, Virgin ran a one-off ad saying if only he had booked Virgin Atlantic, he would have got the limo for free!

When General Manuel Noriega, the former leader of Panama, was extradited by the US Justice Department to Miami for trial, we ran a big picture of him, with the caption 'Only one person has flown to Miami cheaper than on Virgin Atlantic!'

Sometimes the ads were close to the bone, especially when tweaking the tail of our favourite adversaries, notably British Airways. Always irreverent and cheeky, the ads gave Virgin Atlantic a real personality in its early years, which was a key to its success and growth.

Our staff also liked the humour, and the sense of fun. They felt proud to be associated with a company that made people smile and that was seen as a good place to work. We made sure the same spirit ran through everything we did; it was not confined to the cute advertisements. It was crucial that we created an enjoyable atmosphere for crew and passengers alike, at 30,000 feet.

Little touches signified you were on a Virgin flight. Underneath the salt and pepper shakers, modelled on mini aeroplanes, we stamped 'Pinched from Virgin Atlantic'. The butter knife was engraved with the words 'stainless steal'. We put a bar in the Upper Class cabin so people could chat and socialise – after all, travelling should be fun! To entertain our passengers, we were the first to put in seat-back video screens. We served ice cream in the middle of the flights. We did everything we could to lighten the mood and the experience. Over a quarter of a century later, the airline retains that same sense of fun and the ability to surprise and make people smile.

When British Airways sponsored London's Millennium Wheel in the late 1990s, they planned to make a big splash for the official opening and the world's press were there to see it being erected. On the day the wheel was to be raised, the engineers had great trouble lifting it. We jumped at the chance to cause a stir. We scrambled a small airship – it helps to have an airship company – to drag a banner across London's skyline emblazoned with 'BA can't get it up'. It was cheeky, all right, and we, not BA, grabbed the headlines that night.

This sense of humour and risk-taking has infused many of our other businesses. Virgin Mobile Canada produced a series of memorable advertisements poking fun at famous people. When Eliot Spitzer, the former governor of New York, resigned over a sex scandal, where he was identified as 'client No. 9', our ads that week showed a picture of Spitzer with a thought bubble proclaiming: 'I'm tired of being treated like a number.' Another ad in the series showed Hillary Clinton with a thought bubble saying, 'I wish my bill wasn't so out of control.' These ads ran for only short periods of time, but they were picked up in the media and raised the profile of the company and the service.

Over the years I have launched our companies while dressed in some ridiculously silly costumes to amuse our staff, our partners and the press. I have thrown myself off tall buildings, hung off bridges, had tea on the top of a hot-air balloon, driven tanks into Times Square and plunged (usually involuntarily) into oceans – all to grab attention and reinforce a sense of fun.

All of it has definitely made an impression and infused that 'Virgin fun' into new ventures. While it is not enough just to be the joker in the pack, if your service and product excel, then making people smile will help you establish a place in their hearts as well as their minds.

So try taking yourself and your business less seriously. You may be surprised that many others will take you more seriously.

THE PERFECT PITCH

'Have plan – Need money!'

Banking is one of many industries where in too many cases any semblance of good customer service has gone the way of the dinosaur. As such, it is an industry that needs to be shaken up by a company that's ready to take a fresh, new approach.

By no small coincidence therefore, we recently bought the British bank Northern Rock, which we're rebranding Virgin Money. Our goal is not only to provide better customer service, but to return banking to its place at the core of a community and as the engine of the local economy.

When badly run, banks have a negative impact on business growth and development. In 1984 I remember arriving home from Virgin Atlantic's maiden flight from London to Newark and finding our bank manager sitting on my doorstep, waiting to tell me that the bank was planning to close us down after the weekend. It was Friday. Fortunately, we rang around our suppliers and managed to deliver enough funds to the bank on Monday morning to avert the crisis. By Wednesday, we had changed banks.

Flash forward to the present and what seems to be a perpetually tough economic situation. Entrepreneurs who are looking to raise money – whether from banks, angel investors or venture capitalists – face tough conditions. Your best bet is to keep it simple, and be sure that your new business presentation touches on these five key areas:

I. What's in it for them?

Occasionally, an entrepreneur hoping to launch their first business puts so much thought into the concept that he or she neglects the financial and legal plan – and unfortunately, this often becomes apparent early in a meeting, when an investor can lack clarity in what exactly the proposed deal is going to look like.

Before you set up any meetings, gather your team and decide on your goals for your business and how much capital you need to inject to achieve them.

Will you accept money in exchange for a stake in the business, or does it make more sense to take out a loan? What conditions are you willing to have tied to those investments? How much in terms of shares of the company or of its future profits would you be willing to give up in return for start-up financing? Your potential financiers will likely ask these questions, so be ready to give clear, well-reasoned answers.

And as you prepare your presentation, remember that your future backers will want to know how soon they can expect to see a return on their investment as well as possible 'exit strategies'.

2. Be concrete

Winning the trust of an investor means demonstrating a thorough knowledge of your concept or industry and laying out your step-by-step plan for offering something that's new, innovative and will deliver healthy returns on their investment: aka 'ROI'.

Explain how you will turn your great idea into a terrific service or lay out your manufacturing plans in detail. Demonstrate how your approach will provide this for less than people are willing to pay, therefore covering your costs and turning a profit.

Look them in the eye and inject lots of positive language like, 'we will deliver' and avoid wishy-washy phrases like, 'it is hoped that', 'this should with luck' or 'could well result in'.

3. Be unapologetically disruptive

Emphatically explain how your new company will give your customers a better deal than your competitors. And if you think you don't have any competitors, think again. If there is true potential for your concept then you can count on someone else rapidly jumping in to try and exploit the same opportunity.

If a bank or other investor is looking at your business they have almost certainly looked at your competitors as well. In your presentation, therefore, it's imperative that you understand your competition and irreverently explain why your business will do better. Blow them away! Avoid being overly negative. At best, you will seem humourless and self-important, and at worst, like you don't take your competitors seriously enough.

4. Prove that growth is sustainable

There will forever be new markets and new sectors emerging as things change and old businesses reach the end of their life-spans. Nothing stays the same for long, so explain how you plan to tackle the inevitable technological changes and market shifts that are heading your way.

Infinite growth may be impossible in a world of finite resources: so discuss your challenges in terms of resources and waste, and present a plan that inspires confidence in your new venture's ability to sustain the community and the environment.

5. Demonstrate bench strength

Do you have the team in place to take your business forward for the next decade, and do their CVs suggest that they'll be up to the job? Show prospective investors that you have found the right people to work at your new company. Your backers will want to know their money will be in good hands. You also need to show that you have someone on the team who can take over from you the day you decide to move on to your next brave new venture!

The gloom about the global economy means your competitors may be scrambling to hold onto their customers. This is a great time to offer an innovative approach – at Virgin we are seeing an upsurge in innovation and new ideas. There are investors and banks that realise this and, if pitched the right way, are still willing to take risks.

So be assertive, keep your pitch confident, concise and clear and you may soon be seeing that unforgettable first investment cheque. Good luck!

THE OPPORTUNITY OF RISK

And the importance of an escape hatch

To many people, the number and variety of businesses that the Virgin Group operates is unusual: we're involved in everything from music to railways to alternative fuel and even space and sub-oceanic travel. People often ask me to explain the rationale for our group's approach, especially how we decide which sectors and countries to invest in. The answer comes down to our distinct approach to risk.

In life, I have always believed it's better to stick to a few simple values and aims; the same holds true for business. One guideline that we rely on is that if a new business has the potential to damage your brand in any way, you should not invest in it.

At Virgin, when we assess a new business opportunity, our first step is to submit it to our 'brand test'. We are constantly bombarded with new and exciting ideas that 'might' make a lot of money, but if they fail the brand test we will politely decline and move on. For example, we wouldn't start a cigarette company or a 'defence' contracting business. After all, life is short and we all want to enjoy the ride.

Two related guidelines are deeply linked. We feel strongly that there is little point in entering a new market unless it gives us the chance to really shake up an industry. Almost all Virgin's new ventures come from our thinking up a product or service that we believe people really want. Then, if our entry has the potential to make waves, we're going to look at it very closely.

You'll notice that making a profit hasn't entered the picture yet. It's rare for me or the team to consider only the money that can be made. I feel it's pointless to approach investing with the question 'How can I make lots of money?' No one will ever agree on exactly how to make money. The consultants will perhaps say your idea will work, while the numbers guys (aka accountants) can always find a bunch of reasons why it will not.

When it's time to decide whether or not to go ahead, I have always found that the best decisions come from your instinct or experience. If you pursue your passions, your visions will be more likely to become successful realities.

I learned to follow my passions at the beginning of my career, when I created *Student* magazine to give a voice to young people who were campaigning to stop the Vietnam War. As for the actual business aspects, such as paying the bills ... well, we had to sort that out later. We just hoped that we would sell enough copies to stay afloat and learn the business side as we went along.

With almost every venture we've entered since then, we made the move because we spied a gap in the market. Our airline business is a classic case in point: before we entered that industry, I had been travelling a lot because of Virgin Music and often found the whole experience to be lacking, if not downright distressing. I felt we could improve it by focusing on service, on the quality of the flight experience and by adding some fun touches. It worked.

Over the years, my colleagues and I have developed quite a reputation for risk-taking. It's true that we have been fearless about taking on new businesses, sectors and challenges even when the self-proclaimed experts told us that we didn't know what we were about and would be lambs to the slaughter.

But while, to all appearances, we do have an unusually high tolerance for risk, our actions always spring from another principle: always protect the downside. Something I think should be a guideline for every entrepreneur – or for anyone involved in business ventures.

For example, when we made our move on the airline business, I set myself one condition: in our negotiations with Boeing, I stipulated that we could hand the plane back at the end of the first twelve months if the business wasn't working. I was prepared to take the risk but, if it didn't work out, I wasn't going to let it bring everything else crashing down. My colleagues at Virgin Records would still have their jobs and a company to run!

We've made other bold moves into (for us) uncharted territory – mobile telecommunications, financial services and health clubs, in countries all over the world. We just make sure we always have a way out if things go wrong. You have to protect your people. It's your people who make a company exceptional or average.

So, if things don't work out, don't hesitate: take that escape hatch. That way, when all's said and done, you will be able to gather your team, discuss what did or did not happen and then embark on your next venture together. Not much older but a lot wiser.

PRIVATE SPACE
A new Virgin territory

For a long time, the horrific Space Shuttle *Challenger* disaster of 1986 appeared to have ended our dream of space flight ever expanding beyond the preserve of government-funded missions and a few highly trained explorers.

While people of my generation, who grew up in the sixties, believed that the moon landings signified the beginning of a great expansion in space travel – just as the trans-Atlantic records set by John Alcock, Arthur Whitten Brown and Charles Lindbergh marked the beginning of the era of air travel – those dreams were shattered by the deaths of the six crew members and Christa McAuliffe, a schoolteacher who was the first non-astronaut to join a space mission.

At last, however, technology is about to change all that. Virgin Galactic and a small group of privately funded rivals are on the brink of launching a new space age. Together with Scaled Composites, our engineering partners, we are developing a low-energy access system that will be capable of propelling ships into space for a fraction of the current cost. By launching ships from the atmosphere rather than from the ground, we will minimise the impact on the environment, and some day make the trip into space almost as commonplace as crossing an ocean is now.

Most industries have gone through tremendous changes in the last forty years, and space travel is long overdue for a similar overhaul. A single shuttle launch costs around $1 billion. Even launching a small, 400-pound satellite (the size of a washing machine) costs an incredible $30 million or more. Which severely hampers our ability to access space for industrial purposes.

Eliminating this cost barrier to the development of industry in space is vital as the continued exploration of space and development of related technologies will be one of the keys to humanity's survival over the coming century. Satellites that monitor changing weather patterns and their impact will help us to deal with problems caused by overpopulation and climate change, such as food shortages – early warnings to farmers in affected regions will help to save crops and conserve resources. While some first steps have been made in this area, there is a great deal of work ahead.

Today we have the capacity to use off-planet solar panels to generate power, which can be used on the earth below and also to power industry in space – server farms, for example, and some factories and manufacturing plants. A second industrial revolution of this nature will help us in the battle against climate change, removing both the need to generate power and some significant sources of heat and pollution. Sadly, this advance has been delayed by our reliance on expensive, non-reusable launch systems designed half a century ago.

This is where so-called 'space tourism' comes into the picture. Still in its pioneering days, the new space race has become the catalyst for private industry to develop new technologies and delivery vehicles. Virgin Galactic's space ships will increase the safety of the trip to space while significantly lowering the cost and the environmental impact. To date five hundred wannabe astronauts have put down more than $50 million in deposits, providing part of the justification for our investment of more than $450 million in developing Galactic's unique system of air-released space planes.

Our astronauts come from all walks of life. Ranging from artists and scientists to entrepreneurs and financiers. They share one dream: seeing the planet and experiencing weightlessness while helping to pioneer a new approach to space travel.

This is not an easy project. To aid the effort, in 2004 in the USA the Bush administration enacted legislation to set up a regulatory framework that will ensure we develop safety standards that inspire the confidence of the world. In time, other governments will do the same.

Virgin Galactic is not the only company designing new launch systems. Elon Musk, chief executive and chief technology officer of Space X, is currently developing a new ground-based rocket that will be capable of revolutionising the economics of shuttling to the International Space Station. Other companies may enter the market in order to fulfil the need to protect the environment by moving industry off-planet.

Space travel isn't just the stuff of science fiction or something that might happen in the distant future. It will help us to develop practical solutions for some of the biggest problems humanity faces, and that, combined with our innate curiosity, will inspire all of us to quite literally reach for the stars!

THEY SAY
Third-person problems

I have always found that an instant barometer to the state of any company's employee relations is the way their people use the words 'we' and 'they'.

You ask a salesperson for an item and he says, 'Sorry, they decided not to carry that brand any more.' Or you get to the front of the check-in line at the airport and the airline agent tells you, 'Sorry, they have just cancelled that flight.'

This mysterious anonymous entity 'they' is held responsible for limitless problems. Bad news tends to be delivered in the third-person plural, whereas good news is much more likely to be relayed in the first-person singular. I wish my old English teacher could read this, as he was convinced I never listened to a word in those lessons!

So if the requested item is in stock, the salesperson will likely reply, 'Yes, I have that.' When a flight is on time, the agent will say, 'I would like to announce the on-time departure of flight 123.'

Managers and business leaders should watch for this tendency. A company where the staff overuse the word 'they' is a company with problems. If employees aren't associating themselves with their company by using 'we', it is a sign that people up and down the chain of command aren't communicating – and if that turns out to be the case, you'll usually find secondary problems throughout the company, affecting everything from development to customer service.

A company's employees are its greatest asset, particularly in service-based operations where your people are your product. When a company fails to grasp this simple business tenet, the result is invariably an oppositional 'us and them' divide between management and front-line staff.

Listen for complaints from the front line such as 'They [management] are a bunch of idiots who never ask for our opinion on anything' or 'If they had only asked us, we would have told them that their new square peg doesn't fit the round hole we operate in!'

Meanwhile, from managers and executives, you might hear: 'They [employees] just don't seem to get it. Don't they know that square pegs are all the rage with our customers these days?'

Just as two wrongs have never made a right, these two conflicting 'theys' will never make a 'we'.

Resolving the underlying issue is not that difficult. If employees feel they are on the outside looking in – so far outside that they refer to their company as 'they' – then who's to blame? Managers and executives may be investing no effort in making staffers feel like valued insiders. For example, try asking employees where they learn about new products and other important company news. If the answer is the newspapers or a next-door neighbour, then they are truly stuck in a 'they say' quagmire.

Repairing an 'us and them' environment is a cultural challenge that usually calls for greater employee involvement and improved internal communications from the executive suite all the way to the shop floor. In my experience, middle management is a good place to look for the source of the problem. Feedback from up and down the chain often hits a wall in the person of a mid-level manager who has fallen victim to the 'knowledge is power' syndrome. Identifying such blockages and unclogging corporate arteries will bring huge payoffs.

At all the Virgin airlines for instance, if we are creating a new aircraft cabin we will always have the marketing, design and management teams involved from the very beginning. Representatives from the product delivery group (aka cabin crew) will work alongside them, as the crew will ultimately be responsible for the success or failure of their new work environment. In the absence of such input, you risk the crew walking into their new multimillion-dollar cabin for the first time and saying, 'Hmm. Nice, but where's the trash compactor?' Such retrofits can be very expensive!

Involving every relevant employee group in development not only drives better product design but also adds a huge pride-of-association factor: 'We came up with this as a team.' Everyone wins, including customers and shareholders.

This 'us and them' problem is endemic to corporate life and Virgin is no exception. When someone on our team tells me, 'Sorry, Mr Branson, but they don't have that any more', my standard response is, (with a smile!) '"They"? Oh, I'm sorry, I thought you worked here.' Tough love, maybe, but it certainly gets the point across!

This problem is exacerbated by our reliance on impersonal digital communications technologies. One of a leader's greatest challenges these days is getting people to actually talk to each other; one-on-one meetings and old-fashioned brainstorming are vital to the success of any growing business. Sending an email with an attached PowerPoint presentation to a hundred people may be effective in some situations, but most of the time nothing beats gathering all the contributors to a project, soliciting everyone's input and then acting on it.

So, rather than sending that email to the product team, why not walk over there now and talk to them. I am sure 'they' will thank you for it!

A PERFECT 10

There's no such thing

I know that I drive people mad by refusing, point blank, ever to rate their work or new product ideas a perfect 10. No matter how brilliantly conceived something may be, I have always firmly believed that it can always be improved. On the 'Bransometer', a nine is as good as it gets.

There's an inherent danger in letting people think that they have perfected something. When they believe they've 'nailed it', most people tend to sit back and rest on their laurels while countless others will be labouring furiously to better their work!

I have always been an extremely picky consumer. Unlike most 'problem customers', however, I just love it when I am on the receiving end of really bad service. No, I'm not some kind of market-masochist; it's just that some of my best business ideas have stemmed from experiencing bad service.

My first retail business grew out of my constantly being chased out of record shops when my only crime was trying to spend my precious pocket money. We opened the very first Virgin Records shop in London, determined to create an environment where kids (our customers) would want to hang out.

Back then teenagers would spend hours over a single espresso in the pre-Starbucks genre coffee bar. This inspired us at Virgin Records to throw a few beanbags around the place, crank up the volume and transform the music-buying experience into a fun trip. It's interesting that the big bookselling chains took another thirty years to catch on to the same notion!

The trick is always to look at your business or brand from the outside in. Instead of looking strictly through the prism of the latest quarterly financials, attempt to see yourself as your customers see you.

Start simply: call your own customer service line. Just finding the number can be interesting. See how long you hold for, and if you're subjecting your customers to some kind of electronic hell, redesign the system – pronto!

My close associates know that saying, 'Oh, come on, Richard, that will never work!' is like waving the proverbial red rag in front of a bull. Knowing this, they have no doubt used reverse psychology a few times to get me to buy into some crazy notions. But the fact that something has never been done doesn't necessarily mean it can't be done. Often it simply means that no one has been crazy enough to try it – usually for fear of failure.

Around the Virgin companies there really is no such thing as a dumb idea – at least not until we have examined it to see if, with some tweaking, it might be workable. Getting ahead of the curve can require improvising with short-term alternatives that fall well short of that nearly perfect nine. For example, at Virgin Atlantic in the mid-1980s, rather than wait for seat-back video screen technology to be perfected, we went out and bought hundreds of Sony Video Walkmans. Remember those? We loaded up on the latest movies on DVDs, handed them out to our fliers and, bingo, we were the first airline with personal movies.

Our approach had its flaws. The batteries frequently expired before the movie finished, but that was no reason not to be the first to market. Within a year or so, when seat-back technology got to an acceptable level, we were the first airline to feature personal screens at every seat. No one remembered the early hiccups.

Getting the jump on trends requires taking risks and having the confidence to go with your gut. For instance, when we announced that our first Virgin Megastore in the United States would open in New York's Times Square, even New Yorkers thought we'd gone mad.

'Richard,' I remember an American friend saying, 'you're going to lose your shirt. No one in their right mind ever goes there.' There was that red rag – again!

By the conventional wisdom, he was of course absolutely correct. Compared to the more fashionable locations available, Times Square didn't rate even a four. But we had a good vibe about the place, and its less-than-salubrious reputation also meant that the price was compelling. At the risk of making a very public and embarrassing mistake, we went for it.

When it finally opened, our big, beautiful Virgin Megastore was unlike any music store New York had ever seen. It immediately became the talk of the town and, like its sister store on Champs Elysee, Paris one of the city's biggest tourist attractions. It was exactly the kind of retail catalyst the whole Times Square neighbourhood desperately needed and Times Square quickly went from 'sleazy' to 'fashionable' as others opened up.

If we'd taken the safe approach and waited for the area to reinvent itself, we would never have become the centrepiece of the busiest two acres in Manhattan.

Being in Times Square boosted our brand awareness far beyond the store itself. The giant Virgin logo, flashing 24/7 above the storefront, became an impossible-to-miss backdrop to countless movies and TV shows – not to mention millions of tourist photos.

It was a big risk, but one with an even bigger return.

Don't be afraid to take calculated risks. Sometimes they turn out to be less dangerous than the sure thing. Come to terms with the fact that the perfect 10 simply doesn't exist, and, when you hit the nine mark, don't stand back and admire your handiwork. Start work on the next generation to make it still better.

There again, thinking back to the movie 10, maybe Bo Derek proves there is an exception to every rule!

IF YOU NEVER MAKE MISTAKES

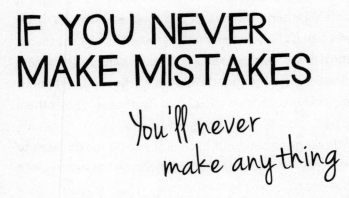

You'll never make anything

There is no better way to learn how to succeed in business than to learn from mistakes – yours or someone else's. I often come across case studies looking into how and why certain companies smashed records, busted budgets and succeeded beyond all imagination. Those studies have their uses, of course, but it's the stories of businesses that didn't turn out so well that especially interest me. I learn much more from them.

One of the reasons Virgin's enterprises have been successful over the years is that we empower our staff to make mistakes – and then learn from them. Since our management structure is totally decentralised, our teams are challenged to run the businesses as if they were the owners. I have found that this creates a high level of loyalty, devotion and innovation. When things do go wrong, the team members feel such ownership of the enterprise that they usually roll up their sleeves and turn it around.

This ability to bounce back after a setback is probably the single most important trait an entrepreneurial venture can possess. If innovation is at the heart of your business, obstacles come with the territory. How you react to and navigate those hurdles will make the difference between failure and success.

I've been lucky enough to be at the helm of many successful companies, but I'm the first to admit that I've also directed a few that failed. You may have heard of Virgin Cola, a company we formed in the 1990s to take on the world's most iconic brands, Coca-Cola and Pepsi. We attempted to shake up the market in true Virgin fashion, but it didn't quite work. Its initial success was so overwhelming that we woke up the two giants of the industry and they did everything they could to squash us.

We certainly didn't lack for enthusiasm, but unlike our battle with BA, we did not have a product that was massively better than theirs. Taking on two such Goliaths, both of which proved to be anything but complacent, was a tremendous lesson for all of us. But still, one of my fondest memories is of our publicising Virgin Cola's attack on Coke by driving into Times Square in a huge army tank with smoke billowing from it and taking aim at the Coca-Cola billboard!

A more recent example involves Virgin Money (our financial services arm) in Australia, where we introduced our first Virgin-branded credit card in 2003. The Australian banking industry is monopolised by four major concerns: ANZ Bank, Commonwealth Bank of Australia, National Australia Bank and Westpac Banking Corporation. Altogether, they handle 80 per cent of all the country's banking transactions. Though we entered the market for the right reasons, had a terrific product, and were a great success with the public, we had entered into a bad deal with the partner bank that issued our card, which eventually led to the business's demise.

Many customers were sad to lose the brand on their card. As a matter of fact, when I'm in Australia I still meet people who carry their old Virgin cards in their wallets!

Which brings me to the next stage: bouncing back. Nearly three years after the failure of the original Virgin credit card, we returned to Sydney to relaunch a range of card products and to start the Virgin Saver online savings account. The difference this time: we have the right people and the right partner (Citibank) for achieving long-term success.

I suppose the secret to bouncing back is not only to be unafraid of failures but to use them as motivational and learning tools. Setbacks are discouraging, but you should always try to channel that feeling into positive action. The key to Virgin's continuing success has been this simple idea: when we get something wrong, we try to understand why and quickly make a change. Then we focus on what works and take it to the next country or industry or sector.

There's nothing wrong with making mistakes as long as you don't make the same ones over and over again. Conduct a thorough postmortem and use the findings to your advantage to make sure you get it right the next time around.

THE CUSTOMER'S ALWAYS RIGHT

Except when he's wrong

What to do when an angry customer calls and asks, unreasonably, that your company redo their costly order? If you are an entrepreneur launching your first venture, you might be tempted to fall back on the common misconception that 'the customer is always right' and make a decision that will pull funds from your hard-earned war chest.

But in my experience, going along with the crowd is rarely a good choice. The expression about customers' infallibility was coined in the early 1900s by Henry Gordon Selfridge, the founder of the eponymous London department store. It has endured because it sounds wonderful to marketers, but most established companies have learned from experience that it is way too all-encompassing to apply in everyday business. In truth, the customer is only right most of the time – after all, they're only human.

I once wrote, 'since your employees are your brand ambassadors, their needs should come before your customers'. That doesn't mean that your customers' opinions aren't important, but simply that you should not build your customer service system on the premiss that your organisation will never question the whims of your clients.

No matter how well you run your company, there are always going to be a few chronically unhappy customers who cost more to maintain than to lose. One of my heroes in the aviation business is Herb Kelleher, the legendary founder of Southwest Airlines. There are many wonderful stories about Herb but I have always loved the one about the woman who was one of the low-cost carrier's most frequent fliers – even though she constantly complained about the service. The more she flew, the more she complained, until, finally, Southwest's head of customer relations sent one of the woman's outpourings to Herb, with a despairing note that read, 'This one's for you'.

Herb's response to the customer was brief: 'Dear Mrs X, We will miss you. Love, Herb'.

No one is sure whether she ever flew with Southwest again, but she never sent them another nasty letter. What's more, the customer service staff probably heard this story within hours and you can only imagine what a boost it was to their morale.

The irony is that many entrepreneurs think that they are upping their company's level of customer service by pursuing a 'the customer is always right' approach, when in fact they end up doing quite the opposite, damaging relationships between customers and staff. If you take away your employees' ability to negotiate on your company's behalf, some will end up at your customers' beck and call – even when they know of a better way to resolve a dispute.

This is an especially important issue for entrepreneurs introducing an innovative product or service to a market. Since creativity and game-changing innovation are two of Virgin's most important brand values, we are aware of the risks involved. One is that no matter how dissatisfied some people may be with the product or service they are using, change is anathema to them. If you are introducing something that's radically different, it's important not to confuse these reflexively negative reactions to change with real rejection.

Try to prepare your customer service staff for what's coming by looking at your product-offering from the customer's perspective. Keep in mind that consumer expectations are severely limited by the scope of their past experiences – most customers cannot tell you exactly what they want. When we started Virgin Atlantic Airways, no potential customers ever said that they'd like to see a new airline offering video screens at every seat or on-board massages. Why? Simply because no other airline had ever provided such things! Will your customers have trouble recognising the upside of the unfamiliar product or service you are offering? What problems can you anticipate?

When clients start contacting your customer service team, use their feedback and your team's insights to understand why some people are having trouble adapting to the change. Look for creative responses and solutions, which may involve anything from an informative marketing campaign to additional technical assistance.

The key to providing great customer service is for your management team to recognise the true worth of your front-line staff, the most talented of whom are expert negotiators with deep understanding of interpersonal relationships. Make sure that they have the tools they need to exercise those skills – that they all have the information they need and they can work with real autonomy to find fair resolutions to the issues that come up. (No scripts!)

There is no maxim that sums up our attitude to customer service as neatly as Selfridge's. Over forty years of launching new products and services, we have always gone to great lengths to listen very carefully to what our customers think they want and then set about giving them something that is often very different, but always a little better.

If your business proposition is innovative, your ultimate goal has to be 'The customer always thinks that **we** are right'.

BRAND AWARENESS

Build it don't gild it

The conventional wisdom at business schools is that you stick with what you know. Of the top twenty brands in the world, nineteen ply a well-defined trade. Coca-Cola specialises in soft drinks, Microsoft in computers, Nike in sports shoes and gear.

A glaring exception in this list is Virgin – and the fact that we're worth several billion dollars really bothers people who believe that they know 'the rules of business' (whatever they are). We're the only one of the top twenty that has diversified into a wide range of business activities, including airlines, trains, holidays, mobile phones, media, the Internet, financial services and health care.

I am proud to be able to say that we have created more billion-dollar companies in more sectors than anyone else.

Between 2000 and 2003, Virgin created three new billion-dollar companies, all from scratch and in three different countries. Virgin Blue (now Virgin Australia) took 35 per cent of the aviation market and reduced fares dramatically. Virgin Mobile became Britain's fastest growing network. Virgin Mobile in the United States was one of the country's fastest growing companies ever, private or public.

As a result of this diversification, Virgin has been able to weather the storm of the global recession that began in 2008. Our risks are spread over many companies, industries and countries; and the failure of one will not bring down the whole group.

Why, then, are business teachers telling young entrepreneurs to stick to what they know, rather than advising them to imitate a company like Virgin?

Because they should. The Virgin brand came into existence gradually, with each forward step reflecting what I was fundamentally interested in. And, to my own surprise, it wasn't publishing magazines, as I'd originally thought; it wasn't even music. My driving force, I realise now, was finding new ways to help people have a good time – ideally, in places where they were least expecting it. Such as airports.

Contrary to appearances, Virgin is highly focused: our customers and investors relate to us more as an idea or philosophy than as a company. It's all about the Virgin experience and the ongoing challenge is to make sure that this experience is consistent with its expectation levels across all sectors. It's all about the brand.

If you are embarking on a new venture, how should you envisage and develop your brand? Let's start with a quick sketch of what a brand does.

Brands exist as a means of communicating what to expect from a product or service. Subscribers to a magazine or newspaper expect a certain perspective and subject matter; families look forward to taking their kids to see the new Pixar movie, regardless of whether it's about animals, toys or cars.

The Virgin brand tells you that using this credit card is rather like using this airline, which, in turn, is rather like using this health club, staying in our hotels and paying into this pension fund. It is a guarantee that you'll be treated well, that you'll get a high-quality product that won't put any surprise dents in your bank balance, and you'll probably get more fun out of your purchase than you expected.

Should you follow the Virgin formula and focus your new company on providing a certain customer experience? It really depends on the type of business you are in. We are in consumer-facing sectors where service is key. You need to assess what is core to yours.

When you are creating your first ads, designing a logo and reaching out to potential customers for the first time, you may be tempted to create a brand that's very corporate and remote. Too many companies want their brands to reflect some idealised, perfected image of themselves. As a consequence, their brands acquire no texture, no real personality and no public trust.

In contrast, Virgin wears its often self-deprecating sense of humour on its sleeve. It has to do with our wanting to be honest about the ups and downs of our business and to share what we think with the people who matter most to us – our customers. The people who see our ads are the same people who read about our tussles, our setbacks and our mistakes. So why would we want to pretend the real world doesn't affect us?

Whatever you and your team decide that your new brand will stand for, you will have to deliver on that promise. So when you're having these discussions, be honest about what it is you're offering.

It is far better to underpromise and overdeliver than vice versa. Superlatives-laden ads for mediocre services and products are the norm with way too many operations. Promise only what you can deliver, and then deliver everything you promise plus some. That's the only way you'll ever control your brand.

And beware: brands always mean something. If you don't define what the brand means, your competitors will. Apple's ads contrasting a fit, happy, creative Mac with a fat, glum, nerdy PC tell you all you need to know about how that works.

So, what's next? For any business building a consumer brand, speaking to journalists is part of the deal. Be prepared! Know what you stand for and be certain that you're delivering it. Then you'll be able to answer every question openly and frankly, building your relationships with your customers and the media.

STEVE JOBS

An entrepreneur who thought different(ly)

When Steve Jobs died in October 2011, many commentators wondered whether Apple, the company he co-founded and led through many exciting years of profit and innovation, could continue to thrive without him.

After struggling with cancer, Jobs stepped down from his post as Apple's CEO, yet his impact on the company remained profound. After all, Apple's innovations – from the personal computer to the iPod, iPhone and iPad – radically changed the way the world communicates and plays. Following Jobs' sad death at just fifty-six, many argued that Apple's future might now be in doubt.

This debate got me thinking about leadership and whether there is one right way to build a great company. Comparing my own experiences at Virgin and Jobs' at Apple was illuminating, since we both built our companies over the past five decades, but we did so in very different ways.

Jobs' ideas about how people should interact with technology and his single-minded pursuit of that vision led him to create a company with a culture that combined obsessive attention to design with highly inventive technology. Computer use was limited to industry and business until he and his team introduced the Apple II in 1977, which transformed computing and our daily lives.

Apple also led a revolution in the music industry when the company introduced the iPod and iTunes in 2001; while the later release of the iPhone and iPad fuelled the creation of a whole industry of application developers. Jobs' passion for great design was the foundation of what is now one of the world's most respected brands.

When my friends and I were building Virgin, we had to approach things very differently, because our vision was founded not so much on a product, but on service. Our culture arose from our constant engagement with our customers and each other. This led us to build a company devoted to customer service and staff engagement; to providing great value and maintaining a sense of fun in everything we do – and our company has gone on to open hundreds of businesses in many different industries.

Steve Jobs tended to be autocratic, taking a top-down approach, while I have always believed in the art of delegation – one of my primary roles is finding the best possible people for Virgin and giving them the freedom and encouragement to flourish. When I set up Virgin Records, I even moved out of the office and set up my desk in a houseboat. My thinking was, and still is, that if you are not always available it forces other people to call the shots, which in turn improves their own leadership skills, builds their confidence and strengthens your business and leaves you with more time to innovate.

So how is it that our very different paths have both resulted in the creation of successful companies? I believe it comes down to pursuing our passions – we both truly enjoyed and believed in what we were doing. Because you are far more likely to be persistent, inspired and dedicated if you love what you do, and if you eventually make something you are truly proud of that filters down to your staff and your customers. This was true of Steve Jobs, and for this reason, despite our vastly different styles, he was always the entrepreneur whom I most admired.

Looking back over Steve Jobs' life, he never lost sight of his love for the company he founded, despite being ousted from Apple in 1985. Once outside Apple he transferred that energy, investing in and leading a small company called Pixar, which achieved stunning artistic and technological feats and transformed the field of computer animation. When he was asked to return to Apple in 1997, he led the then flagging company to new heights, and continued working throughout his illness. For me, leading Virgin has been my great adventure: challenging, exciting and creative, this is something I would do if there were no money in it at all.

Sometimes pursuing your vision means that you will have to ignore others' warnings and even jeers. I have written about my decision to start Virgin Atlantic and then Virgin Australia:

so many of my decisions have gone against the advice of industry analysts, management gurus and sometimes my closest advisers.

In Jobs' case, the products he and his team envisioned were so different that the stock price usually dropped after one of Apple's products was first introduced to the public, because shareholders and 'experts' were so certain that the company was headed in the wrong direction. This happened most recently with the release of the iPhone 4S, and again it was an aberration – sales of the device have since broken all previous records at Apple.

As you pursue your own entrepreneurial vision, take heart if building your company involves overcoming obstacles and ignoring your critics. Pursue your passion; admit it when you encounter something you are not good at, and either delegate it or find a way around it (even Jobs hired great professionals to lead public relations efforts, and he famously formed alliances with Apple's competitors, IBM and Microsoft); and when things go wrong, pick yourself up and keep going. This is an adventure that takes courage and conviction.

Throughout his life, Steve Jobs encouraged everyone he worked with as well as his customers to 'think different'. And while you might take issue with the grammar, it is certainly fundamental advice that every entrepreneur should take to heart.

FIRST IMPRESSIONS ARE HUGE
But don't blow it with the second

My mother used to urge me to put on clean socks and underwear every day, reminding me, 'You never know if you're going to get hit by a bus.'

The implication was clearly that she didn't want to suffer the humiliation of hearing an emergency room nurse say, 'Doctor, quick, take a look at this. I don't know when this boy last changed his underwear!'

This shows the importance of making a good second impression. Setting aside the 'impression' that the bus would make on me, the medical staff would have their first impression of me upon my arrival at the hospital, and the second impression during the examination, as they learned more about my personal hygiene.

In business, creating a favourable impression at the first point of customer contact is an absolute imperative.

Despite the fact that everyone knows this, many companies still only manage to do a mediocre job at best.

But what clearly isn't widely understood is that in a world where so many transactions are conducted online, the customer's second impression of the brand can be even more important than their first.

The second interaction an online customer has with your business usually involves something that has gone wrong – they're having trouble using the product or service. Handled correctly, this is a situation in which a company can create a very positive impression. Sadly, it's where things often go terribly wrong.

One of the biggest mistakes I see on an alarmingly regular basis is companies burying their customer service phone numbers in their websites' deepest, darkest nooks and crannies. Clicking the 'Contact Us' tab is just the first step in a tricky game of 'find our phone number if you can'. Surely customers are supposed to have their 'Aha!' moment when they're using your product, not when they finally succeed in unearthing the company's contact information!

Most callers to customer helplines around the world are greeted with some variation of what's surely the most absurd statement ever recorded: 'Your business is very important to us. Please continue to hold.' Some companies even make it worse by adding friendly snippets like 'Your anticipated wait time is twenty-three minutes'. But the subliminal intent of this message is 'We are not really interested in retaining your business if it means we have to staff up to serve people like you. So use our website, will you?'

If some customers have the staying power to wait until a real person picks up the phone, the aggravation is far from over. Before customers are granted an audience with a real person, they usually have to key in their account numbers at least once. But when a representative finally picks up the phone, the most common greeting is: 'Can you please give me your full name and thirty-seven-digit account number?'

Websites are not designed to avoid such irritations either, and often make negative second impressions. Take the account registration process, for instance. It's sensible for an online banking service to require users to choose a secure password and user name, but this step seems ridiculous to someone who is trying to buy a pair of socks. While the registration process is an important tool in building mailing lists, if it frustrates your customers, what's the point?

Most airlines (Virgin included) provide passengers with the option of checking in via a self-service kiosk – the company's chance to make a good second impression, since the first contact is usually the online booking process. This device will check passports, issue boarding passes and in some cases even print out baggage tags. If the process goes well, it makes a reasonably good impression; not only do these devices (digitally) greet customers by name, but they're seldom impatient or surly. But, still, it's best always to have human help on hand to assist customers when the process goes awry. And with all the complexities of national and international flights, you can be sure this will happen!

In the hotel industry, the check-in process remains the exclusive domain of human beings, with uniformed receptionists responsible for a customer's second impression of a brand. I have never worked out exactly why, but most luxury hotel chains have bested the airline industry when it comes to doing this well. It's no coincidence that the term 'hospitality industry' is understood to encompass hotels and restaurants, but airlines are conspicuously excluded.

Managers and executives who want their companies to make positive first and second impressions must learn to balance the web's labour-saving efficiencies with real human beings who can help when things go wrong. One reality check I perform on a regular basis is to test-drive our own websites to see how long it takes me to find that elusive customer help number. Try it, and if you have to dig through more than a couple of screens, then maybe the website design needs to be rethought.

Consider the customer relations value in putting a simple no-nonsense big 'Need Help?' number on your homepage. By making that human help too hard to find, to paraphrase the title of one of my books, you're taking a risk that the customer might say, 'Screw it, I won't do it.'

TO WIN THE WAR ON DRUGS
End the war on drugs

People seem to have forgotten that, decades ago, crime generally wasn't a good way to make a living: it was after the drug war began that pop culture started to portray drug dealing as a route from poverty to riches. But only a few actually become wealthy, and as *Freakonomics* authors Stephen J. Dubner and Steven D. Levitt showed in their 2005 book, many street dealers live with a parent and take part-time jobs to make ends meet. Other studies have shown that many of these exploited workers are hard-core addicts themselves.

To cut off the flow of money to the top criminals, all we have to do is call a halt to the drug war and decriminalise the use of illegal substances.

The war on drugs funnels money to exactly the wrong people: when public officials pursue a tough-on-crime agenda, narcotics dealers profit as drug prices go up, while demand remains the same. This is an industry that earns a staggering

$300 billion each year, and, with that sort of money at stake, criminals will do anything to outsmart the law: move their drug manufacturing operations to countries where authorities can't pursue them; buy heavy weaponry (as in Mexico); infiltrate government agencies (as has happened in many nations, from Peru and Bolivia to part of West Africa); kidnap and intimidate police, politicians and civilians. Criminals get rich while ordinary people pay the price – both in terms of higher taxes and, sometimes, with their lives.

In a world where the drugs problem only gets worse – an estimate by the UN shows that consumption of opiates worldwide, including heroin, increased by 35 per cent between 1998 and 2008 – it's difficult to imagine criminals reduced to looking for proper jobs. In some Latin American countries the drug cartels are challenging the authority of the government – some of their militias are better equipped than the military, and the gangs have been known to provide communities with security and basic social assistance. In Afghanistan, a fair proportion of the money flowing to the Taliban comes from the sale of opiates. The US Drug Enforcement Administration says that al-Qaeda agents in North Africa, West Africa and Europe have funded their operations through the drug trade.

Until recently I felt, as many people do, that the war on drugs was the best policy for our society. But I changed my mind soon after joining the UN Global Commission on Drug Policy along with former UN Secretary-General Kofi Annan, Javier Solana, the European Union's former foreign policy chief, former Brazilian President Fernando Cardoso, and many others. Our findings clearly show that the global war on drugs has been nothing short of a well-intentioned but incredibly expensive mistake.

Our commission found that in countries where drug addiction was decriminalised and instead treated as a public health problem, there were decreases in crime, decreases in the number of addicts and improvements in overall public health.

Portugal, for instance, decriminalised the use and possession of drugs in 2001 and has not sent one person to prison in the last 10 years. By setting up clinics where heroin users have access to needles and methadone, along with medical treatment for addiction (which is much cheaper and more effective than prison), Portugal reduced its number of users, especially among young people and addicts. The number of new cases of HIV (from dirty needles) was down by 70 per cent between 2000 and 2009, and, as an interesting side benefit, researchers also reported a significant reduction in household burglaries.

As we assess new businesses opportunities, our team at Virgin often looks at what works in different countries, studying how we can adapt successful approaches to new markets. In the case of the drug war, our commission has shown that the key is to switch to 'harm-reduction' strategies. One of the more telling studies looked at the situation in Switzerland, which switched from a law and order approach to public-health-focused policies in the eighties and nineties.

According to research by the University of Lausanne: 'Heavily engaged in both drug dealing and other forms of crime, [hard-core problematic users] served as a link between wholesalers and users. As these hard-core users found a steady, legal means for their addiction, their illicit drug use was reduced as well as their need to deal in heroin. ... By removing local addicts and dealers, Swiss casual users found it difficult to make contact with sellers.' The addicts, who are often both users and low-level dealers, but whose need had been reduced by medically prescribed heroin, had been the crucial link between suppliers and casual users.

Imagine that in your country addicts are not being jailed but treated at clinics. Imagine that their numbers are declining. That police departments have ended their efforts to round up low-level dealers and some of those officers are now focusing on organised (and random) crime. Many have been freed up to work on community policing, because even petty crime by addicts is on the decline. Imagine that the additional public funds are being spent on health and social programmes rather than on law enforcement and prisons. That, just like when Prohibition was ended in the United States, the black market has dried up and the drug gangs have withered away. Imagine that money and power are no longer associated with drugs and crime, and the media, and even our culture, are changing in response.

How do we take a stand against crime? By treating drug use as a health problem not a criminal problem. By eliminating the drug dealers' connections to their markets. So let's pull the plug – and save lives. As business people, if one of our policies is failing we will cut our losses quickly and change tack. It's extraordinary that governments continue to pursue the same, failed policies, decade after decade, with all the misery these policies inflict.

SCIENCE: THE LAST FRONTIER

A Nymph in Atlantis

As a kid I read Jules Verne's *Twenty Thousand Leagues Under the Sea* and was enraptured by its sense of adventure and mystery. Since then I have spent a lot of time with oceans – floating over them (and occasionally crashing into them) in balloons, and speeding over them – but little time actually under them.

More than two-thirds of the Earth's surface is covered by water, and yet humankind has hardly explored the vast expanse of saltwater that surrounds us. The wonders of space have been charted in far greater detail.

Countries such as the United States have invested trillions of dollars in searching out faraway planets and solar systems. We can land on the moon and circle the world in a space station, but we still lack the capability to reach the deepest parts of the ocean or withstand the immense pressure that such a dive would entail. There is no sign that things will change any time soon as governments remain relatively uninterested in deep-sea exploration. .

The deepest a modern submarine can go is 22,000 feet below the surface, and yet there are trenches in the Pacific that are more than 37,000 feet deep. To make such a journey – going deeper than the height of Mount Everest – we need significant technological breakthroughs in materials and design. The filmmaker James Cameron set a new world record in March 2012 diving 5.1 miles beneath the ocean waves in his submarine *Deepsea Challenger*.

Only two private companies are seriously researching these futuristic submarines – ourselves and James Cameron. James' craft is very heavy and can go up and down to capture samples. Ours has much greater manoeuvrability and will be able to explore for miles. The two crafts compliment each other perfectly and we are discussing embarking on adventures together. It is a classic Virgin venture, full of adventure, fun and the desire to establish a new market.

Every great adventure begins with that first step and ours has taken the form of the Necker Nymph, a new three-man sub based at my Necker Island home in the British Virgin Islands. The Nymph has been designed especially for us, and it will 'fly' to about 130 feet below the ocean's surface – performing twists and turns. Submarines like the Nymph will allow a passenger to track and view the wonders of the ocean without having to be a trained diver.

Much of the best ocean viewing is 100 feet down. The amazing Nymph can dive and loop like a plane and will allow our passengers to keep up with turtles, dolphins, whales and giant spotted eagle rays – like the one I saw recently while swimming off the beach on Necker.

Granted, 130 feet is just a little shy of 36,000 feet but it's a start, giving mere mortals, not Navy Seals or scientists, a first chance to begin exploring the underwater world. In time the Nymph will be followed by new generations of subs able to get w-a-a-y down, further than we've ever been before.

In conversations with many of our Virgin Galactic customers, who are planning to go into space, I have found another common interest: exploring the oceans' uncharted waters. Most are as intrigued as I am by the dark depths.

I believe we can learn a lot from these voyages. We will find new species and better understand the make-up of the deep-level waters. We will also be able to monitor and track more accurately man's destruction of certain areas. To organise an effective campaign to preserve our planet, we must learn how our actions affect the oceans and how quickly we are destroying them.

The oceans were rich with life when I was a child but, sadly, are much less so today. We need to treat them with respect and nurture the life there. Good farmers understand the land and the need to leave certain fields fallow so that they can be replenished. The same goes for oceans and sea life. I have been told that the pirates off the coast of Somalia have had an interesting impact on the waters they call home. I am not advocating piracy as a solution, but these 'rubber-boat-buccaneers' have scared off the deep-sea fishermen, allowing the surrounding waters to be replenished with a wide variety of sea life. It will be interesting to see if the impact of overfishing can be detected by our fleet of new submarines in deeper parts of the ocean.

Why start our voyages from Necker, my Caribbean island? Apart from being a beautiful location from which to explore local sea life and coral, the island is just a few miles from the Atlantic's deepest trench, the Puerto Rican Trench. This stretch of water has never been explored, and I hope within a year to have travelled to the darkest depths of this great sea valley farther down than Everest is high.

For me, there are echoes of the great explorers from the era of Sir Francis Drake – the men who first discovered the Virgin Islands. I am keen for our submarines to emulate the feats of Drake and chart the deep local waters acre by acre, trench by trench, valley by valley.

As an added bonus, we may even find treasure. The Caribbean is littered with shipwrecks, many laden with bounty from South and Central America. Some say there may be more treasure and gold below the sea than above. I have a map showing more than two hundred shipwrecks within twenty miles of Necker. Some may be lurking in relatively shallow waters, hidden by the years; others may be much further down. We will be looking for them, especially now we have developed our submarines to go all the way down.

As I look over the ocean from my hammock on Necker, I am incredibly excited by the future opportunity to look *under* it. Besides discovering new species, (they sat 80 per cent are undiscovered) charting the trenches and finding treasure, we may even find the lost city of Atlantis ... you just never know!

PS In Jules Verne's book, the 'twenty thousand leagues' refers to the distance travelled, not the depth. Just as well when you consider that 20,000 leagues is more than six times the diameter of the Earth!

CHOCKS AWAY

Let them have at it!

This may sound like a truism, but it has to be said: it takes an engaged, motivated and committed workforce to deliver a first-class product or service and build a successful, sustainable enterprise. Empowering employees so that they can make good decisions is one of an entrepreneur's most important tasks.

This means that you must build a corporate comfort zone in which your people can confidently express themselves and display the courage of their own convictions. From the business's first days, you must ensure they aren't constrained by an overly rigid structure, micromanagement or overregulation. While guidelines are useful for establishing a framework for the tasks ahead, a hard-shelled setup will hinder creativity and risk-taking. It will instead quickly lead to mindless repetition, lack of motivation and a falling off in standards.

If you can encourage and trust your staff to use common sense, you will find that over time their solutions to problems will become more innovative, rather than less so. Make sure that experimentation is encouraged and employees aren't afraid to make mistakes. In fact, your goal should be more than merely encouraging your employees to use common sense. Ultimately, you want their approach and solutions to become entrepreneurial or, more accurately, intrapreneurial.

One of many intrapreneurial teams within our group is led by Les Payne on Virgin Australia's engineering and maintenance staff. He keeps an eye on all aspects of ground safety, including the wooden chocks used to hold plane wheels in place when they are parked at the gate. About five years ago, he noticed that in heavy rain the chocks did not stay in place, and that this equipment also wore out quickly.

Les and his colleague Ian Scott decided to redesign the chocks. They soon hit on a more durable and environmentally friendly material: plastic that had been recycled locally. The price would be the same as the traditional wooden ones, but the chocks would last at least six times longer.

Over time, we have been replacing the one thousand timber chocks in use across the Virgin Australia network with the recycled plastic version. We were so pleased with this simple but effective measure that we reported it in internal newsletters, drafted memos to help raise awareness and also feted Les and team at the Virgin Group's Stars of the Year dinner for successfully demonstrating how helping the environment can also help the bottom line. In 2006, both Les and Ian received an industry award for this achievement as well.

The steps to constructing a creative and free-thinking workplace are quite simple, but it really has to start at the top. CEOs need to lead by example, by being visible and approachable in their role as the lead creative problem-solver. Give out your email address and phone number, listen carefully to employees (as I frequently point out, I always carry a notebook so I can jot things down), follow up on all problems, act on the best suggestions and celebrate others' creative milestones and intrapreneurial achievements.

When Virgin was small and housed in cramped offices, it was much easier for me to keep in touch with employees, but nowadays I have to rely on a team of dozens of chief executives who drive forward the various businesses within the Virgin Group as our ambassadors and advocates for the Virgin culture we have created.

Whether you are running a small company or a large one, there are employees you may not get to speak to often, and whom you must rely on others to supervise. Things to look for in your managers: do they give out their contact info? Do they have little black books of their own? Can they tell you about employees' good ideas and which of the best ones they acted on? Do they promote intrapreneurship within their teams? Are they intrapreneurs themselves?

Such switches are very helpful in broadening senior team members' experience and helping them to remember that getting things done the conventional way is not necessarily the best way. When your top managers are true intrapreneurs, you can be sure that you are on your way to building a committed, engaged, creative workforce guided by common sense and a spirit of adventure.

Chocks away!

LIKE A FINE WINE

Ageing brings many benefits

I am, as I said in the Introduction, a huge fan of Australia and Australians. Australia always strikes me as a young and vital nation so it is interesting that the following question came to me from Down Under.

> **Q:** **In Australia there is often an overt bias against employing older workers. In a recent business magazine article, a recruitment consultant stated he doesn't look at anybody over thirty-five.**
>
> **These are some of the preconceptions often aired: older workers can't change; they are not as creative; they can't think laterally; they are not open to learning; they cost more to hire.**
>
> **What is your approach to hiring older workers? If you were looking for a position, how would you look to overcome the ageism barrier?**
>
> **– C. Goldsworthy, Australia**

A: Whoever that recruitment consultant is they deserve to be looking for a job themselves for making such a ridiculous confession. It is an especially appropriate time for me to address the issue of age and the workforce. I know this fact will surprise you (says he with tongue planted firmly in cheek) but I myself recently turned sixty.

The same year that I hit the big six-oh I also ran my first ever marathon and not only finished it but did so in just under five hours. In the same year I tried to set a record as the oldest person to kite surf across the English Channel; however, high winds (and waves) forced me to abandon the attempt – but I'll be back!

Challenges such as these were once associated with younger people but nowadays people are living longer, much more active lives, so retiring at a relatively young age is no longer necessary. If people look after themselves with regular exercise and a good diet, there is no reason why they shouldn't keep going forever: my grandmother played golf almost every day of her life and recorded a hole in one at the age of ninety!

I certainly plan to continue to work until I feel that I'm no longer making a real contribution to Virgin. I see a good thirty years of work ahead of me. It's true that in my sixties there are some tasks that suit me better than others, but I see few real limitations to continuing in my current role.

In the UK, the government has recommended extending the age of retirement to sixty-seven, and many countries in the rest of Europe are contemplating similar legislation. It is not just governments, but company boards around the world, that are now facing the challenges of serving ageing populations.

So while it is certainly true that some employers may have negative preconceptions about hiring and retaining older workers, they are only doing themselves and their businesses a disservice. Entrepreneurs and managers who hope to succeed are taking a close look at older applicants.

Studies have shown that, contrary to popular perceptions, older workers actually have fewer time-keeping and absentee issues than do younger employees within a business; they also tend to have higher levels of commitment to their jobs and loyalty to their employers, which reduces staff churn and helps to reduce recruitment costs.

And there is a strong business case for companies to diversify the age groups they employ. In all our ventures, we put a real emphasis on offering great service, and, to succeed, we must truly understand our customers and see our service through their eyes. As our and others' customer bases get older, managers will need staffers who mirror these changing demographics.

This is a challenge for Virgin since we have tended to be quite young at heart. Currently, the average age of the group is still fairly young, with more than a third of our staff under the age of thirty-five and only around 3 per cent over fifty-five years old.

This is largely determined by a few factors, including the sectors that we operate in and the newcomer status of some of the businesses. For example, Virgin Active, our health club chain, attracts a younger workforce due to the physical nature of the work. As the challengers of established brands, our airlines – Virgin America, Atlantic and Australia – have tended to be magnets for younger cabin crews and ground staff. These employee groups consist of such large headcounts that it does somewhat skew the overall average age of the Virgin group of companies. Even our finance business has younger staff – again, people interested in the company's challenger status and also in new product development. But as we prepare for the future, this is a factor that clearly needs to change.

How? Well, many businesses retire their experienced staffers, both to cut costs when times get tough and as a matter of course. But those companies risk losing a lot of key skills when workers with a wealth of knowledge and experience leave the business.

One answer is to become more accommodating in work arrangements. Offering part-time jobs, job shares, flexitime and full-time jobs with longer holidays may attract older workers. This would enable everyone – and not just older employees! – to strike a better work–life balance and allow companies to retain their skills, experience and make a team for the newer generations.

I hope that with this approach our group will continue to maintain a very open policy of recruitment and that *ageism will not be an issue. Hiring older workers isn't just the right thing to do; it also makes good business sense.*

WHAT'S IN A NAME?

Maybe more than you think

Q: Why were Virgin Blue aeroplanes painted red?
– Dick Percs, Australia

A: The name and the distinctive red planes were based on
a play on words, but there is a lot more to the old Virgin
Blue name than the colour, so let's start this story at the
beginning.

As I explained, we came up with the Virgin name one
evening when discussing our new record shop idea.

We instantly loved it for many reasons, not least of
which was that, even after the swinging sixties, the word
was still somewhat risqué.

Virgin had a fresh, sexy feel to it; it declared that we
were new to the music industry, and the business world in
general. We excitedly scribbled it down with a big capital V
– that scribble became the basis for the Virgin logo.

The original Virgin name turned out to be successful on many levels: It was unique, so it was instantly recognisable; it was memorable but not specific to one industry or region; and it was compatible with the brand that we would eventually build. We were lucky. These days, some entrepreneurs pay branding specialists a lot of money to create, test and refine a brand name and logo – but that's no guarantee of a successful outcome. Any entrepreneur choosing a company name should think carefully about whether a proposed name is sufficiently versatile to be extended to future products and services. Virgin Records worked well in the entertainment industry, but we were not at all sure of ourselves in 1984, when we painted our company's logo on the giant tailfin of Virgin Atlantic Airways' one and only Boeing 747. It stood out – by that time we had chosen our distinctive shade of red.

Not everyone loved it. David Tait, one of the original group who set up the airline, gave me a tough time, declaring, 'Nobody's going to fly on an airline that won't go all the way.' But I dug in my heels and insisted it was better than 'British Atlantic Airways' – the original name of our start-up company – pointing out that the world really didn't need another 'BA'.

That fledgling airline became the foundation on which we built Virgin's brand values and consolidated its international presence. Virgin Atlantic was soon a market leader because of its innovative approach, and because we provided great customer service and terrific value. Our distinctive marketing was always edgy, irreverent, self-deprecating and fun. As we said at the time, 'with a name like Virgin you can't take yourself too seriously'! In any case the word spread quickly and the airline's success facilitated the launch of an extended family of other Virgin-branded companies all over the world.

Our unique name and brand, along with a consistent execution across every trading unit, made the company a success. As we introduced the various businesses that followed, we ensured that Virgin always represented added value, improved service and a fresh approach, from Virgin Money to Virgin Galactic. We knew, as did our customers and competitors, exactly what we stood for.

So, finally, let's get back to the story behind the name Virgin Blue. In the 1850s, a large influx of immigrants arrived in Australia, hoping to make their fortunes in the gold fields. The Irish, many of whom were redheads, soon gained a reputation as hard drinkers and fighters. A fight, in local slang, was a 'blue'. When a redheaded Irishman passed by, people would say, 'There goes a blue', and to this day Australians often give their redheaded friends the nickname 'Bluey' while 'blue' is the general equivalent to 'pal', 'mate' or 'buddy'.

In 2000, when we were preparing to launch the airline in Australia, an Australian chef on Necker said to me 'Why not call it Virgin Blue?'. He suggested that Aussies would connect our upstart nature and the traditional red logo with the name Virgin Blue. To highlight the play on words, we painted the planes a bold red. Following its strong domestic start, Virgin Blue became an international airline, and it now flies to the Middle East, many Pacific Island nations and North America – countries where the blue versus red wordplay is not understood. So in 2011, we renamed Virgin Blue and our other airlines in the region, uniting them all under the banner Virgin Australia.

If you find yourself in a difficult spot because of your company's name – perhaps because business has expanded in different directions to what was anticipated – don't panic. Try looking at other solutions; consider incorporating your old name into your new one. This could be the perfect opportunity to reintroduce your company to the media – tell them about your plans and your renamed business's core values.

In our case we got lucky. While 'Slipped Disc' might have been a fun name for our record label, I am not so sure it would have worked quite as well for airlines or fitness clubs!

SO, YOU WANT TO BE CEO?

Be careful what you wish for

There is nothing quite like the early, frenetic days of an ambitious start-up. It's high-octane and high-risk; the shared experience builds tremendous team spirit and camaraderie that will help your people through some of the company's most trying times. Your team will seldom work harder than during this period.

The launch stage is also an ideal time for you to decide whether you are suited to the CEO position. While entrepreneurs have the dynamism to get something started, and often create opportunity where there was none, not all of them are good at running businesses. Recognising your own weaknesses is essential to your company's future.

Once your business matures, it will almost certainly become more challenging to maintain the excitement that accompanied the 'rah-rah' days of the launch. It will then be up to you and your team to make sure that employees remain motivated.

This is the point at which you will have to make a decision about which role is right for you: entrepreneur or manager?

If you're hoping to continue as CEO, you must learn the ins and outs of every area of the company. There are no shortcuts – getting this right requires patience and hard work. When Brett Godfrey was CEO of Virgin Blue (now Virgin Australia), he insisted that all senior managers learn every job at the airline, including luggage loading. (I needed to visit the osteopath for a checkup after my stint!) This will prepare you to delegate properly as your business gets bigger. When people come to you with problems, you will be able to provide practical advice based on your first-hand knowledge of how the business works.

You should also sign every cheque and examine every invoice at least every six weeks; you'll soon know where the money is going, how it moves across your organisation and where it is spent. When you are familiar with the company's everyday finances, you'll find yourself asking: 'What on earth is this cheque for?' You may be able to cut unnecessary expenditure dramatically. Even at the Virgin Group, I continued this exercise for many years, signing every cheque that went out for one month out of every six, and I ask our managing directors to do the same.

Most importantly, a manager must have the acute psychological know-how to smoothly organise a large group of people and handle the pressures of an ongoing venture. Use the launch period to gauge your own strengths and weaknesses as a leader; ask your best advisers for their honest opinions on your performance. Consider how you inspire and motivate other individuals to cooperate and get the job done.

It takes a certain generosity of spirit to fairly judge people's merits and limitations, and to trust them with responsibilities. Optimism, openness to possibilities and self-confidence are all qualities of a good manager. Some people are more inclined to these qualities than others – which describe you?

Are you someone who brings out the best in people? Great managers seldom criticise their team members. Just as plants need water, people need encouragement so that they can grow and flourish. An employee who makes a terrible error of judgement rarely needs to be told about it, so instead his manager should focus on helping them learn from their mistake and recover their confidence.

Do you acknowledge your own mistakes and apologise for them? You'd be amazed at how much people appreciate this quality in their supervisors, and how much they can learn from their managers' experiences. The ability to recognise your own missteps and discuss them is crucial, and requires bravery. If you promoted someone and they are not performing well, you should be able to discuss the problem with the employee, admit your mistake, offer them their old job back and see them through the transition – a difficult conversation and a situation that not everyone is equipped to handle.

Management is also about communicating clearly; explaining why a decision has been taken or in which direction the business is going. Your communications should carry authority without being hectoring or bombastic, presenting a simple vision of what has to be achieved. At the same time, good managers continually question the way people do things and encourage employees to do the same – thereby ensuring they are always ready to adapt to changing conditions.

While a natural talent for the CEO role is truly an asset, many leadership skills can be learned. If there are areas you need to work on, ask yourself who among your circle of friends and colleagues is a leader you can learn from, and talk with that person frankly about your wish to improve. The mentoring experience may be deeply rewarding for both of you.

At the end of this process, if you and your advisers agree that you are suited to the role then you may decide to stay on as CEO and help your business grow. If you perform better in the role of entrepreneur instead, then you need to find a suitable senior manager to take your place. Look for someone who has the above qualities, and, when you find your replacement, give them a proper stake in the business.

Now, it's time for you to move on and set up your next enterprise. So what's it going to be?

THE CHINESE PLATE TRICK

Share the spinning

Q: Virgin is a large company with many diversified businesses and a culture of delegating. How do you avoid breakdowns in communication and ensure that good decisions are made? Another question I have to ask is how you deal with the hundreds of emails you must receive? What's the secret?

– Shezad Virji, Kenya

A: *Reading through recent emails, I was struck by the number of questions from readers about how to better manage their own time as they go about the task of running their complex businesses (and lives).*

As a successful business matures and expands, bureaucracy usually starts to take hold and members of the senior management team can easily find themselves overwhelmed by the sheer number of meetings and volume of correspondence. At this stage, an entrepreneur faces the challenge of how to effectively manage this new structure – it's kind of like mastering the Chinese plate trick – and it's a transition that has been the undoing of many enterprises.

First, let's look at how to manage your own time, the first step in managing the complexities of a business. On average I receive about four hundred messages a day, so effective time management is a huge issue for me. I'm aware that some senior executives simply delete all emails from people they don't know personally, arguing that such messages just create an unwelcome distraction. To them, it is not worth the effort of weeding out these uninvited emails to find which, if any, merit attention. I find this approach to be impolite and bad for business.

Recalling the time when I was just starting out and needed advice, I try to respond to as many reader emails as I can. When I'm not on the road, I always try to allocate some time to read through the list and dictate quick answers to my assistants, pass some to my colleagues, and usually write a couple of longer, more detailed responses myself. This is the most effective way of dealing with my inbox, and while doing so, I learn about trends that may affect Virgin businesses or about problems that may warrant my attention.

You must manage your BlackBerry; do not let it manage you! Way too many executives check their smartphones throughout meetings and during their *off-hours. Apart from the fact that it's tantamount to rudeness in a meeting, it isn't good for anyone's concentration and has a negative impact on decision-making. Show the little gadget who's the boss in the relationship! Use it only in bursts: check emails for an hour or so and then put it away, so that you can focus on the task at hand.*

When you're thinking about how to manage not just your own time, but all your employees', the key is to enable everyone to stay focused. I have become much more aware of this in recent years, as I have invited groups of entrepreneurs to meetings on Necker Island, where expert speakers discuss issues such as climate change, poverty and peace. I often spend some time talking about my experiences, hoping to share lessons that will help my guests, many of whom find themselves managing that transition from scrappy start-up to established company.

The advice that entrepreneurs seem to find most helpful at this stage: give the rest of your team space to work – in many cases, by moving your office out of the building. Physically remove yourself from the business's day-to-day functions and, if it's not already the case, find someone to replace you as head of operations so that you will have enough uninterrupted time to look at the big picture and plot the company's future direction. If you don't break up the workload, you and your team are more likely to find yourselves struggling to manage the complex and competing responsibilities of running the business today instead of determining strategies for tomorrow.

You must be sure to hire great people who you can trust to run your business. But remember, no two people do anything exactly the same way and your replacements will not do everything the same way you would have. And everyone – yourself included – makes the occasional mistake, but you must resist the urge to snatch back control. This is the only way to instil a true sense of responsibility; it will prompt your senior management team to run the business as though they own it themselves.

I often speak about the advantages of staying small, which is one of the Virgin Group's strengths in terms of communications. Our many small businesses require less bureaucracy, and so our people are more likely to know who is doing what and why.

You can build good communications into your company's DNA by ensuring that discussions are built on openness, unambiguous language and a demonstrated willingness to listen to everyone who has something to say. And by everyone I mean everyone – from the person at reception to your top managers. Make sure that people's curiosity is encouraged and watch it grow. If they have made good suggestions and have seen results in the past, your staff will ask questions and be persistent, which will help them to solve any problems they encounter.

This will free you up to focus on the big picture: to dive in when you see an issue that needs your attention, to help senior management to sort out a crisis, to lend your expertise when executives are swinging a deal and, importantly, to deal with those emails from people seeking advice or with complaints, either of which may turn out to be a source of inspiration!

HOW TO BAKE AN ENTREPRENEUR

First take one intrapreneur

I am incredibly lucky to be able to live in the British Virgin Islands, one of the most beautiful spots on the planet. Necker Island is our home, my office and a luxury resort all rolled into one.

An amazing coincidence, I know, but I had nothing to do with the Virgin part of the name. Christopher Columbus stumbled on the place in 1493 and gave the islands the fanciful name of 'Santa Ursula y las Once Mil Virgenes'. As intriguing as that may sound, thankfully over time it has been condensed and anglicised. I'd have a hard time telling people I live in a place called 'Saint Ursula and the Eleven Thousand Virgins'.

One of the first of many charming things visitors to the BVIs will see is a sign in the airport immigration hall which, rather than the customary 'Residents' and 'Nonresidents', reads 'Belongers' and 'Nonbelongers'.

I've come to find the term 'belonger' amazingly powerful. When a nation embraces its own as 'belonging here', as opposed to just living there, it breeds a wholly different form of loyalty. It reminds us that this is where we belong, and so our efforts are not just on our own behalf, but also to benefit the community.

This set my mind to wondering (something an office hammock enables much better than a straight-backed chair) how such little, seemingly semantic, details apply in the business world: what if companies had belongers rather than employees? Does what we call each other make a difference in other contexts?

Over the years I've been called a lot of things, many of which are not fit to repeat here! The (polite) handle I get most often these days is 'entrepreneur'. I remember having to look the word up in the dictionary after a newspaper article about my first business venture, *Student* magazine, described me as 'a budding entrepreneur'. At the time it sounded pretty cool – 'a person who initiates and organises new commercial enterprises, usually involving considerable risk', according to my dictionary.

These days, all kinds of people claim the title 'entrepreneur'. On the other hand, a title that hasn't received nearly the amount of attention it deserves is entrepreneur's little brother, 'intrapreneur': 'an employee who is given freedom and financial support to create new products, services and systems, who does not have to follow the company's usual routines or protocols'.

While it's true that every company needs an entrepreneur to get it under way, healthy, innovative growth requires a smattering of intrapreneurs who drive new projects and explore new and unexpected directions for business development.

Virgin could never have grown from *Student* magazine to the hundreds of companies it is today were it not for a steady stream of intrapreneurs who looked for and developed opportunities, often leading efforts that went against the grain. One example that springs to mind was at Virgin Atlantic, about fifteen years ago. None of the big expensive seat design firms seemed able to solve the design problems posed by our specifications for our Upper Class cabin, but a young inhouse designer, Joe Ferry, volunteered (insistently) to give the project a go.

We set him loose, and the unorthodox herringbone-configured private sleeper suites that resulted from his 'outside the box' creativity put us years ahead of the pack and made for millions of very happy horizontal fliers.

How to unleash the power of intrapreneurs like Joe? The key is to enable them to pursue their vision.

But people don't always think of leaders within a company – the managers, executives, and the chief executive officer – as people who enable others. As I learned back when I was starting up *Student* magazine, 'The chief executive officer of a major corporation might only make a couple of decisions a year, but those decisions can affect the lives of millions.' What a terrible way to run a company!

So, since this seems to be true throughout the business world, clearly it's time for a major shake-up in the nomenclature of business. What if CEO stood for 'chief enabling officer'? What if that CEO's primary role were to nurture a breed of intrapreneurs who would grow into tomorrow's entrepreneurs?

We inadvertently developed this role at Virgin by virtue of the fact that when we've chosen to jump into a business about which we have little or no real knowledge, so we've had to enable a few carefully selected people who do know which end is up. When Virgin moved into the mobile phone industry we had no experience, so we looked for our rivals' best managers, hired them away, took off their ties and gave them the freedom to set up their own ventures within the Virgin Group.

Perhaps the greatest thing about this form of enabled intrapreneurship is that often everyone becomes so immersed in what they're doing that they feel like they own their companies. They don't feel like employees working for someone else, they feel much more like ... well, I think the only word to describe it is 'belongers'.

Which brings us right back to where we started, in the glorious Virgin Islands, and I'm headed back to the hammock.

CHANGE IS IN THE AIR

Jetting to sustainability

Q: What is your next project concerning sustainable development?

– Emily Lau, USA

A: *The answer is really a host of projects running on parallel lines, but if I had to pick one business that needs a nudge down the sustainability path it is probably aviation.*

The aviation industry is facing a tough and exciting challenge: creating a new way of doing business that uses less energy, relies on renewable sources of energy and minimises or eliminates harmful waste products – beginning with a sustainable commercial alternative to jet fuel. On terra firma, people can choose to buy hybrid and electric cars, buses and trucks instead of gasoline-powered vehicles, but in the air travellers don't have the same options. Whether you board a plane at Heathrow,

JFK or Narita, it will always be filled with kerosene.

This needs to change. From January 2012 airlines are included in the European Union's Emissions Trading System (ETS – a cap-and-trade system that allows companies to buy and sell carbon emissions credits), which will increase costs for those based in Europe. Switching airlines to renewable fuels should be a target in the global fight to lower carbon emissions. We need to find a way to simultaneously lower our carbon output and fuel bills – and right away.

Most people in the industry are now aware that it is possible for planes to fly on renewable fuels. In February 2008, one of our Virgin Atlantic aircraft did a test flight from London to Amsterdam using a fuel that mixed 80 per cent kerosene with 20 per cent biofuel – a fuel that was derived from babassu oil and coconut oil, both harvested from trees on established plantations. At the time, then CEO of BA, and current chief executive of BA's parent company, International Airlines Group, Willie Walsh commented, 'Saying there is a biofuel available is, to me, a bit of a PR stunt. I wont say [biofuels are the answer] because I don't believe it's true.' Other airlines, including Air New Zealand, Continental Airlines, Japan Airlines, KLM and the UK's Thomson Airways have since completed similar tests as well. The real challenge is to scale up production of one or two workable fuels and get airlines around the world to use them. Why do the words 'chicken and egg' come to mind?

How do you tackle industry-changing innovation? It doesn't happen overnight. Virgin made a commitment to 'green' business more than five years ago, deciding that this was an area that would be good for the planet (and hopefully would pay the bills), so we stayed in contact with innovative start-ups in this field and kept up with the latest developments. Around the same time, Virgin Atlantic pledged to make a 30 per cent carbon reduction per passenger kilometre by 2020, and we also committed to developing and sourcing sustainable, renewable fuels for all our Virgin airline fleets.

Over the past five years, Virgin, our Green Fund and I personally have all invested in a number of such initiatives, including ethanol plants in the US and pioneering biofuel companies such as Gevo and Solazyme. Development is a long, complicated process, with many hurdles to be overcome: the need to find sustainable feed stocks, develop the high-performance fuel and then test and obtain certification for the fuel's use in aviation engines.

But breakthroughs do happen sometimes, and in late 2011 we made an announcement about what I believe could be one of the biggest steps forward in my lifetime towards developing a scalable, low-carbon aviation fuel. We believe that a fuel we are developing with New Zealand-based LanzaTech should cut Virgin Atlantic's carbon footprint in half. Simply put: we've entered the recycling business, turning much of the waste from chimneystacks into aviation fuel.

This revolutionary fuel production process recycles waste gases, including carbon dioxide, which would otherwise be emitted into the atmosphere. We're tackling the steel and aluminium industries first: they have a plan in place to capture waste gases from nearly two-thirds of the world's steel and aluminium mills and convert them into jet fuel.

In the meantime, our goal is to have many Virgin Atlantic planes running on the new low-carbon fuel within three to four years, starting with those flying Shanghai to London and Delhi to London routes, then expanding it around the globe.

For years, people have doubted the practicality of using sustainable fuels – it would be great to prove them wrong. Our hope is that other airlines will be quick to follow Virgin Atlantic's example and the industry's carbon footprint will be radically decreased.

Another of our efforts that looks promising is one based in Australia. Virgin Australia has signed a memorandum of understanding with Dynamotive Energy Systems and Renewable Oil to help develop a sustainable aviation biofuel. Our consortium plans to use an accelerated thermal decomposition technology to process mallee, a eucalyptus tree that is grown in many parts of Australia to help control salinity on farmland and that is harvested sustainably. A demonstration unit that will make biofuels for testing, certification and public trials should be up and running next year and a commercial-scale plant could be operational as early as 2014.

It is vital that plans to develop a sustainable aviation biofuel are truly sustainable and bring wider benefits; in this case improving socio-economic conditions for the Australian farming community and helping the environment. We have pledged to develop jet fuel plant sources in a way that minimises biodiversity impacts and doesn't deplete food or water sources. We have also promised never to use high-conservation-value areas or native ecosystems for plant source development, and to reduce total lifecycle greenhouse gas emissions.

I have written frequently about the need to find new ways of doing business, and, at Virgin, our many small steps over the years – reaching out to people who had revolutionary ideas, developing our own and seeing how our companies could work together – are starting to turn into industry-changing innovation.

Too many business people say things like, 'They really should do something about developing alternative fuels'. Well, we decided we simply couldn't wait for 'them' and picked up the ball ourselves. If you are hoping to bring change to your industry, rather than waiting for others why not do the same?

DON'T LIKE THE SECOND OPINION?

Get a third

To succeed in business, you must learn to be a good listener. And then you should learn to bounce every idea you have off numerous people before finally saying, 'We'll give this one a miss', or 'Let's do it'. One of the positive by-products of learning the real importance of consultation and listening in business is that it will benefit many other aspects of your life.

Major medical decisions, for example. When I was twenty-two years old, I was playfully swinging a young girl around, only to have my knee give in. After a couple of days on crutches, I saw a surgeon who told me it was the worst ligament tear he'd ever seen and that he wanted to do a major operation on my knee right away. Though I was young, I already had seven years of business experience, so I knew that at the very least I should get a second opinion.

I made sure that I didn't tell the next surgeon what the first had told me, and I did get completely different advice – but it still involved an operation. I decided to go for a third opinion. I searched out the one group of people that would be sure to get excellent advice: the English national football team. I looked up their number in the phone book and asked to speak to their physiotherapist who, much to my surprise, agreed to see me.

Unlike the first two doctors he thought there was no need for an operation, and if I followed the right exercise programme I'd be back on my feet again in three weeks. Indeed, by the projected date, I was skiing! Almost forty years later I ran the London Marathon at the age of sixty. Would I have been able to run such a race if I'd taken the first advice that was given to me and undergone that major operation? Unlikely, I fear.

Not long ago my wife, Joan, woke up to find that one of her legs had swollen to three times its normal size. Our family doctor told us that he believed she had suffered a major blood clot. We rushed her to hospital, where we were told that she had a series of clots that led from her ankle right up to her groin, and that it was the worst case of such clotting the doctors had ever seen. She was in great danger of a pulmonary embolism, as bits of the clot threatened to break away and travel to her lungs. The doctors put her on a drug called Warfarin, pulled a compression stocking over her leg and told her that over a number of years the leg would gradually improve, but that at any stage she might suffer a major pulmonary embolism that could kill her.

Along with our two children, Sam and Holly (Holly is a trained doctor but also a businesswoman), I wanted to be sure that the doctors had given her, and us, the best possible advice. Surely there had to be a better answer than for Joan to drag around her swollen leg and live with all the inherent risks. We rang up numerous doctors in our search for a solution, and slowly, like detectives, we edged our way towards a much better conclusion. We found a recently invented treatment for Joan that would have seemed like science fiction only a few years ago, but would radically improve her chances of a successful recovery.

The first doctors we took Joan to see did not know much about this method and told us that it was far too risky. But soon, after speaking to a number of experts in the field, we realised that the risks of her current condition far outweighed those of the new approach. So we signed on for the new solution, which was to temporarily put a tiny umbrella inside her leg so that if a clot did break off it could not enter Joan's lungs – a potentially fatal development. During this time, the doctors would also inject the clots to break them down, get the blood flowing again, and drain any stubbornly congealed blood from her leg.

We moved her to another hospital that was willing to carry out this procedure. A mere two days later, she all but skipped out of the building! Her leg was completely back to normal, the clots had disappeared and, apart from having to take Warfarin, she can now lead an almost completely normal, risk-free life. This procedure can only be done within the first ten days or so after the original clot forms. Apart from asking questions – lots of them, and of many different experts – you often need to drop everything and act quickly.

In business, asking questions may not save lives, but it can save you a lot of time and money. Don't impose your own thoughts on the conversation until you've digested all the feedback and feel that you are close to a decision. Don't tell people about others' suggestions until you've heard what they have to say. In the end you may decide that the best advice is to walk away – and later find out it was the very best solution.

You may decide to push on, and it's likely that, after all your probing and listening to others' advice, your original idea may have become distorted almost beyond recognition, but it will probably have improved considerably.

Whatever the outcome you'll have fun learning from other people and the end result will be a lot better if you've kept an open mind and sought out what's right. And if you use this approach in your personal life, it just may help you keep a loved one alive and well for many years to come – one whom you could otherwise have lost.

BREAKING UP

When is it the right thing to do?

Q: What do you do if you have a 50/50 business partnership with a friend, but, after ten years, it no longer works? I don't want to ruin this friendship, but the business is suffering tremendously. He still expects his 50 per cent share. From experience I know that he is not going to improve. What would your view and solution be?

— *P., Australia*

A: *Sadly this is a common and sensitive situation and I frequently receive questions about it. Friends often set up businesses together, and initially their camaraderie and trust serve them well. However, as the business grows larger and gets more complicated, such bonds are easily strained, and yet the constraints of friendship may prevent the founders from confronting the problem and taking decisive action.*

Handled properly, there is no need for this situation to damage a business or friendship. When I confronted a similar situation in 1980, the recession in Britain was having a negative impact on Virgin Music. As sales dropped and the economic outlook worsened, our forecasts showed that the company was going to lose one million pounds that year. Tensions ran high and my relationship with my best pal and partner, Nik Powell, was being damaged.

Nik was one of the co-founders of Virgin Records, and along with my cousin Simon Draper and myself, had been crucial to its early success. But as our financial situation forced us to make tough decisions, we found that we were increasingly at odds over strategy.

Nik wanted to consolidate the business, while Simon – who as managing director ran the label – wanted to expand our way out of our troubles and sign a couple of new acts. Two prospects interested him: Phil Collins and the Human League.

I had added to our difficulties by unilaterally deciding to buy two nightclubs. I felt that the deals were just too good to turn down, even if they added to our already mounting debts.

While Nik ran our record stores well and had produced the cash we needed to expand our music label, I realised that we were not going to get ourselves out of the hole just by increasing the profit margin on sales in our record stores. We needed to do something drastic. We needed to find another breakthrough act.

With the business stuttering and the management team at odds, I had to choose between the two approaches and *decided to go with Simon's. It was a tough call, but it was the right one, even though it meant that we had to dissolve our partnership with Nik.*

Once I had made the choice, we moved ahead quickly. I borrowed the money to buy out Nik and he took with him a couple of the businesses he loved – our film business, for one. When everything was settled, we held our 'divorce party' at one of the new clubs.

Since then, I have done business with my friends in other situations, and, looking back over forty years, the lessons are clear. There is nothing wrong with doing business with your friends – in fact, I encourage it. It's important to create an atmosphere where friends can work together and where friendships flourish. We all spend so much of our adult lives at work, so let's enjoy it.

The big caveat that has to go with this, however, is the necessity to deal quickly with any problems. The fact that your partner is also a friend cannot be an excuse for turning a blind eye.

In your situation, P., you need to confront the issue head-on. You should be honest with your partner about his shortcomings and their consequences, or else these problems will fester. Employees who pick up on the tension may take sides; rivalries may develop. If this happens, your personal relationship – and also perhaps your business – could deteriorate beyond repair.

If the issue is dealt with quickly, honestly and openly, you will clarify for yourself and your employees where the business is heading and why. Once you have made the decision to dissolve your partnership, try to be generous in your convictions – buy him out if you can. If you work out an amicable settlement and provide your partner with a dignified exit, you will then be able to work on your friendship and mend bridges in the years to come.

IF I COULD DO IT ALL OVER AGAIN

I'd do it all over again

One of my favourite sayings is 'Ninety per cent of life is just showing up', because finding the courage to pursue your vision and start a new business often hinges on just that first step.

Once you've spotted an opportunity in a given sector, having the confidence to follow your dream and raise that first crucial bit of financing is often the hardest problem facing a budding entrepreneur. The following two mailbag questions reminded me of how I established some of my first businesses, and how I'd begin again if I had the chance.

Q: If you were twenty-four today and were given a budget of $3,000 to start a business, what kind of business would you choose? What if the budget were around $25,000?

— Alex Bodislav, Romania

A: *That's an easy one. It would definitely be some kind of web-based business, and I'm not sure it would make a difference if I had $3,000 or $25,000 to start out. You can build a very decent website for very little money and the thought and creativity that you yourself put into it is free.*

As I have said before, my career began in the late sixties with my first business venture, Student *magazine. I started by selling it one issue at a time, and selling the advertising from my school phone booth. Then I moved on to music. The publishing and music industries are struggling today due to the changes brought about by the Internet – but where there's upheaval there's opportunity.*

Look at how Apple has revolutionised the music industry with iTunes, its online music store, and the iPod.

I may have indirectly been responsible for iTunes and the iPod, which, ironically, ended up killing our music stores. Back one April Fool's Day, I pulled the music industry's leg. I pretended that I'd set up a giant computer in the UK, where I had stored every music track on every label and that I was about to launch a device called a 'Music Box' that music lovers could use to download any track, wherever they were. The headline in Music Week *was 'Branson's Bombshell: The End of the Industry'. I had music moguls – including Chris Blackwell of Island Records – ringing me, begging me not to do it. At lunchtime, I announced that it was an April Fools. Interestingly, Warner Brothers didn't realise this and spent six months trying (and failing to) catch up. Steve Jobs told me he too read* the story and some years later thought, 'why not give it a go?' The moral of the story is, if you're going to do an April Fool's joke, follow up on it yourself. Anyway, such is the genius of Apple's designs and their hold on the consumer that the company has taken the mobile phone market by storm with its 'you gotta get one of these' iPhones. Then it tackled the publishing world with the iPad.

A whole industry is growing up around designing apps – games, magazines and booking engines – for these devices. Successful app designers and publishers are already making a fortune, the way publishing and music moguls did in the sixties and seventies.

I have always been fascinated by all these forms of content – music, books, television and film. Virgin has invested in all of these industries, with mixed success. If I were reborn as a 24-year-old, I would look at this area for an 'app-gap' – a gap in the market or an opportunity to shake up the leading players.

And today I would also think big: these days an entrepreneur faces few geographical boundaries to success. When I started Virgin, our projects were limited to the UK but the development of the Internet has shrunk the world to a more cosmopolitan, connected and accessible marketplace.

Q: What are the top three ways to find funding for a new business?

– Pavlina Stoyanova, Canada

A: *The first, and probably most obvious, is to borrow from your family and friends. This is high-risk, for if things go wrong you can lose not only a business but also a friend or the friendship of a family member. However, for many entrepreneurs this is the fastest and only way to raise start-up funding.*

Over the years I have been lucky in that my family has been able on a few occasions to help me in a small way. In 1966 I was living in my friend Jonny Gems' parents' basement off Edgware Road in London. We were broke and struggling to get Student magazine off the ground.

But one day my mum, Eve, brought us £100 in cash. She had found a necklace on the roadside and taken it to the police. When nobody had claimed it after three months, the police told her she could have it. She knew we were out of funds, so she sold the necklace and gave us the money. That £100 paid our bills and kept us going for months. That necklace saved our necks!

The second option is to apply for a bank loan. From the beginning I tried to build my businesses by relying on my own resources and some bank debt. This allowed me to control the lion's share of the equity until I felt we had the stable platform we needed to attract outside investors. In Virgin's early expansion days we often lurched close to collapse because I was so reluctant to bring in outside equity. I felt our limited capital kept us focused on finding the next great act, and ultimately this was a real contributing factor to our success.

Lastly, if the bank won't lend you the money on the strength of your idea alone, you have to have the faith and conviction to borrow against whatever assets you have, such as a flat – or, if you are lucky as I was, a friend's or relative's assets.

In the early seventies, I was looking to purchase The Manor, the Oxfordshire country house that would become our first recording studio: the asking price was £30,000 and I had put up £2,500, which represented every penny I had in the world. Much to my amazement I had also managed to persuade the bank to lend me £20,000, which still left me £7,500 short. That is, until my dear old Aunt Joyce stepped in.

It was an amazingly generous and risky gesture, and one that I may not have accepted had I known that she had mortgaged her own house to provide the capital. I did, however, gratefully accept it and bought The Manor, which soon became home to our first hit, Mike Oldfield's brilliant instrumental, Tubular Bells. Virgin grew quickly from those shaky beginnings to become a successful business, and I made sure I paid back Aunt Joyce her £7,500 – with interest – as soon as I could!

There is, of course, another risk in accepting favours from family and friends, which, as any fan of The Godfather will know, is just what they might ask for in return. In my case, had she really wanted to push it, people might today be flying on 'Aunty Joyce Airways' ...

MORE WALKING AND TALKING

Less typing and griping

Why is it so hard to pick up the phone? They are a lot smaller than they used to be, and these days, even non-tech-savvy types like me can call, text and email messages, sending files and photos around the globe with ease. Despite these advances, the quality of business communications has become poorer in recent years as people avoid phone calls and face-to-face meetings, I can only assume, in some misguided quest for efficiency.

I recently heard a senior manager defend his handling of a situation by saying, 'I don't know why they didn't understand the issue. I must have sent a dozen lengthy emails on the subject in the last week.' A brief conversation followed by a concise email to confirm the next steps would probably have settled matters within a few minutes, and saved him the trouble of writing those lengthy emails, and the complications that followed.

Another executive complained to me, 'I've sent the guy a bunch of text messages. I know he's there, so why isn't he responding?' Clearly it would have been better to pick up the phone or walk over to that person's desk and discuss the matter face to face, a move that would have resolved the issue and immediately eliminated the growing tension.

In short, if these managers had tried walking and talking instead of typing and griping, they could have solved these problems quickly and easily, saving themselves time and effort.

Why not pick up the phone? As technology has evolved, so has business etiquette. People tend to rely primarily on email and text messaging because these communications are precise and less intrusive, while a phone call now signals that a matter can't be solved by ordinary means. But there is nothing efficient about allowing a small problem to escalate.

To break down this new barrier to effective communications, make face-to-face employee contact part of everyday life in your office. The Australian term for it is 'going walkabout'; many business management consultants call it 'management by walking around'. Whatever you call it, it works, and if you and your senior staff aren't doing it, you are missing out on one of the most inexpensive and effective management tools around.

I have always enjoyed getting to know people at Virgin companies. I find it a much better way to get a feel for what's really going on than sitting in my office – okay, lying on my hammock at home – reading reports. As not everyone is outgoing, here are a few tips:

Be egalitarian. Don't restrict your walkabout only to your area of the company; try to meet colleagues at (literally) every level – not just on the top floor! Go on your walkabouts at random times – you don't want front-line employees thinking, 'It's three o'clock on Tuesday. He should be here any minute.' If managers or department heads ask to tag along, politely explain that you will get to know people better if you are on your own.

When you meet an employee for the first time, be sure to shake hands and always introduce yourself by name, no matter what your position at the company. Keep it informal: 'Hi, I'm John Brown' is a lot less intimidating than 'Good afternoon. I'm the chief financial officer, Mr Brown.'

Don't restrict the conversation to work matters. If you notice a family photograph on a desk, a comment like, 'I see you have a tennis player in the family? My kids love to run me ragged all over the court' will help to break the ice.

Relax and have fun, ask questions and *listen.* Ask your colleague what she sees as her area's strengths and stumbling points, and listen to her thoughts on the challenges the business faces. Jot down anything that strikes you as worthy of follow-up. (When I don't have my notebook handy, I am notorious for writing reminders on my hands and arms.) If you have any news to share, provide a balanced view – positive developments as well as concerns. It's less likely that shop-floor employees will know as much about the bigger picture, so they may need your help to put matters in perspective. But they will have ideas and opinions that can be every bit as relevant as your own so listen up and take more notes.

Above all, try to catch employees doing something good – recognise and celebrate people's strengths and achievements on the spot. If, however, you stumble on a problem, it's far better to quietly bring the matter to someone's attention later, rather than embarrass the staff member by having the head honcho calling them out in front of their peers.

One boss with no such qualms was Robert Crandall, the legendary leader of American Airlines in the 1990s. Bob used to love using the old dog sledding line that went, 'if you're not the lead dog the view never changes'. The irascible Mr Crandall would seem to have failed to recognise that in business it is the job of the lead dog to go out of his way to make sure that the rest of the team gets to see the bigger picture.

We have found at the Virgin companies that, when senior managers make the effort to foster relationships with employees and colleagues, a real community spirit results. So please get out of that ergonomically correct office chair right now – there's no time like the present for a trial walkabout. It will get easier with practice.

If you need to explain your sudden presence in unfamiliar territory, you can simply say 'Richard sent me' – or then again, maybe not!

ACCIDENTS HAPPEN

Emergency planning cannot wait for the emergency

If death and taxes are the only sure-fire things in life, then the only certainty in business is that one day things will go wrong. If you're lucky it needn't be a catastrophe, but when you first start up a business, one of your priorities has got to be emergency planning.

Put a disaster recovery plan in place that fits your situation: in case supply lines are cut, a hurricane hits or other natural catastrophe looms. Because if disaster strikes, rest assured that a lot of people are going to be looking to you for answers.

On 23 February 2007, at around 8.15 p.m. we were hit with our first real emergency. One of Virgin Rail's new Pendolino tilting trains had derailed in the north-west of England, on a remote part of the West Coast Main Line. Margaret Masson, an elderly passenger, was badly thrown around in the coach as the train slid along the railbed and then careered down a steep embankment.

For ten years, Virgin Trains had safely carried millions of passengers all over Britain. Virgin Atlantic, meanwhile, had flown tens of millions of customers around the globe without a single injury. That night, life changed for all of us at Virgin. Margaret Masson was dead. Several other people were seriously hurt.

I was on a family ski trip in Zermatt, Switzerland, when I received a text message that said there had been a rail accident. After speaking to Tony Collins, the chief executive of Virgin Trains, I hired a car and drove through the night to Zurich, where I got the first flight out at 6.30 a.m.

When I arrived in Manchester that morning, the BBC was reporting that the train was intact, and that had helped to save many lives. That was heartening: all our new trains had been built like tanks for this very reason. A later report, which was confirmed, suggested that a rail track was responsible for the accident due to track failure. Twenty-four people were taken to hospital.

I met Margaret Masson's family in the mortuary at the Royal Preston Hospital in Lancashire. They were clearly devastated, and I offered them my condolences. We found ourselves hugging each other.

Soon I was facing a barrage of television cameras and a pack of journalists who wanted answers. I thought I was going to choke up. I came very close, but kept it together and stuck to the facts as we knew them. At the time, ahead of the official accident investigation findings, there wasn't much I could say other than sorrys and thank yous. I expressed my gratitude to the train driver, Iain Black, who had stayed in his seat at the front of the train as it crashed, doing everything he could to save his passengers, and in the process sustained serious injuries. Our other employees on board had all behaved in an exemplary fashion, ignoring their own minor injuries in order to lead customers to safety.

Why were we able to react so quickly? When Virgin Trains was putting its emergency procedures in place, we had analysed a number of serious rail incidents and had been appalled by the length of time that usually passed before anyone in charge started speaking to the press. Confusion and then blame set in quickly as anxious people waited to find out what had happened and why.

So our disaster planning had prepared us to accomplish three main goals: get senior people to the scene as quickly as possible; be efficient in dealing with the passengers, staff and media; and be honest about what was happening. We knew that those first steps would get communications established so that everyone – passengers, staff and the media – would be able to obtain the information they needed. Even if there was nothing to report, someone had to report it!

Beyond disasters and accidents, as you forge a new path, finding growth areas and innovative solutions to your clients' problems, it's inevitable that you and your team will make mistakes. It is important to recognise this and ensure that everyone in the company is prepared for the worst.

This is one of the reasons you should be keeping the press up to date on what you're doing. Aside from maintaining a high profile for your company, it may someday help journalists put any bad news in context.

Which brings me to the difficult balance that all entrepreneurs and CEOs need to learn how to maintain: always protect your reputation, yet don't be afraid of making mistakes. These rules ought not to contradict each other, but they often do. I've known plenty of talented and trustworthy people whose careers have been damaged by the shadow of past errors, and who have suffered professionally as a result. If you or someone in your company has made a serious mistake, don't be afraid to ask the senior figures in your circle for advice and help. Distinguished people are often generous and understanding, to a fault. (They've been through the mill; they know what life is like.)

Investigate the matter thoroughly; if you can, try to pinpoint where your internal processes failed. During this period, do not keep your head down – that will do you no good at all. Instead, communicate openly with the press and keep them up to date.

Next, apologise. Explain what happened, express your regret and describe what steps you have taken to correct the situation. While some will call for the chief executive's head on a spike I do not think a CEO is always obliged to fall on his sword in most such cases.

Like the Boy Scouts', your company motto should be 'Be Prepared'.

REACH FOR
THE SKIES
It's closer than you think

If you decide to tackle an engineering challenge or to venture into the scientific unknown as an entrepreneur, you're embarking on a real adventure – difficult, fascinating, often risky. Sometimes you and your team might feel quite alone, while at others you might choose to partner with friends or even your competitors. It's important to remember that we all learn from and build on others' accomplishments – as I've written before, an entrepreneur does not succeed alone.

This idea was driven home to me one time when my publisher came to visit me to discuss the next book. I had imagined this would be another project based on my business experiences, but he surprised me when he said, 'There's this great passage in your autobiography where you nearly get yourself killed.'

'Really?' I responded, 'Which one? There have been quite a few!'

Unimpressed he continued, 'Do you recall in the mid-1970s when a chap called Richard Ellis got you to try out his early form of hang glider?'

I told him that I remembered all too well. The contraption was called a Pterodactyl. I took off in it by mistake and nearly killed myself but, tragically, just a few days later Richard actually did kill himself in the thing. 'That's right,' he said, 'Ellis died, and you escaped by the skin of your teeth. What we were wondering was, what on earth made either of you want to take those kinds of insane risks?'

Why? Well, for starters let's not forget that Richard Ellis was one of the inventors of the Pterodactyl Ascender series of hang gliders. A few years after the crash, Jack Peterson Jr flew a Pterodactyl across the continental United States in 120-mile hops. His machine now hangs in the Smithsonian right next to SpaceShipOne, the first private manned space vehicle, which was designed by Burt Rutan.

'Well ...' I began slowly, not exactly happy with where this conversation was going, 'there was the thrill, obviously. It seemed like a great adventure. And then there was the whole sponsorship thing. Ellis wanted me to champion this new form of flying.' And then there was ...The more I talked, the more 'and then there was' connections I uncovered. 'You know hang glider wings are based on a design that was supposed to bring NASA's Mercury capsules down to Earth? This of course ties in with what we're doing with Burt Rutan at Virgin Galactic. Re-entry is the toughest challenge for any space vehicle, and ...'

I stopped. The publisher was grinning.

Soon we had a book, which we titled *Reach for the Skies* in homage to my childhood hero, British flying ace Douglas Bader. It's about flight but much more than that; it's about the people behind the inventions and accomplishments.

If you're considering a project that involves technical challenges, remember that, long before innovators have the right materials at hand, we already know how to achieve our dreams. Look at the history of flight: the workings of intercontinental air travel were being hashed out by textile engineers John Stringfellow and William Henson nearly sixty years before the first aeroplane flight.

Then, the process of engineering those materials will require teamwork, self-reliance and bucket-loads of goodwill. To achieve a nonstop flight between London and Paris, Charles Lindbergh's team adopted working methods that wouldn't look out of place in our spaceship factory in the Mojave Desert.

Throughout my career, I have been deeply involved in projects that have pushed the envelope of manned flight. While I am known for drawing attention to Virgin, none of our experiments were mere publicity 'stunts'; they were steps in our research and development process. Swedish aeronaut Per Lindstrand and I crossed the Atlantic in a hot-air balloon in 1987 and the Pacific in 1991, setting records that still stand. The envelopes of those balloons were made of incredibly high-tech materials as radical then as Virgin Galactic's space-faring composites are today.

Once you've solved all those engineering challenges, you'll have to figure out how you're going to turn your hard work into money. Drawing attention to your new idea or invention helps, but you'll need a business plan.

But this working method, with its components of engineering, adventure, celebrity and business, was not invented by the Virgin team, though it has carried me from a student magazine to the edges of outer space.

This approach drew admiration, criticism and incredulity long before Queen Victoria's parliament rang with laughter at the preposterous idea of a world airline; long before startled peasants took pitchforks to Jacques Charles' gas balloon in 1783. It takes a very long time to build a business. At Virgin, my team and I build for the future. And the future's wild.

SUSTAINABLE ENERGY

The next gold rush

The haunting images of Japan's damaged nuclear power stations after the devastating tsunami that struck the country in March 2011, and the growing concern over rising radiation levels, left me thinking about how the world will power itself in a sustainable, safe way in the future, and how entrepreneurs can develop solutions.

For many involved in the process, the construction of modern nuclear reactors was a step that was already agreed upon in the effort to build a new system powered by sustainable energy. New reactors built around the world would supply part of the energy needed to meet the future needs of rapidly developing countries such as India and China. This, combined with projected advances in technology drawing on solar, wind and tidal power, formed the beginnings of a plan.

A delay in building those plants would force many nations

to increase their use of coal before carbon capture and storage technologies are viable – a serious setback in the global battle to halve carbon emissions by 2050. This is the target that some scientists believe we need to meet in order to stabilise global warming at two degrees Celsius above pre-industrial temperatures.

The word 'sustainable' gets a lot of play these days but what does it actually mean? I use it to describe ways of supplying energy that will remain productive over time and protect ecological diversity; technologies that we can envisage our grandchildren and their grandchildren relying upon. 'Sustainable' describes methods of power generation that help to preserve the Earth's natural systems.

This is where entrepreneurs come in – most of the technologies will be created by start-ups that become small businesses. I don't want to use soaring language here; no one is asking you to save the planet. Just look at the opportunities, dream up a couple of ideas and work on them. The debate about climate change has taught us that no one is going to solve global warming by edict, but local solutions and small initiatives tend to punch well above their weight. In the business of sustainable energy, small is beautiful.

Virgin's research in this field shows that there are many technologies in development that directly or indirectly harness the power of the sun, and their potential is limitless. The almost unbelievable fact is that, in just one hour, the Earth receives more energy from the sun than is consumed by the whole of our society in one year.

Near Rome, the 84.2-megawatt Montalto di Castro Photovoltaic Power Station became Europe's largest solar farm in December 2010. In Spain, the Planta Solar 20 concentrates solar heat in a tower 165 metres high, turning water into steam that powers an electricity turbine, generating twenty megawatts. Solar energy technologies are also rapidly advancing, with companies like Odersun producing thin-film solar cells – our own Virgin Green Fund is an investor.

Wind energy is developing quickly in the United States, where wind farms are starting to match the output of some big power stations – the Roscoe Wind Farm in Texas produces 780 megawatts, exceeding the 550 megawatts that is generated in a typical coal-fired plant. In the United Kingdom, a consortium of companies is building the London Array, an enormous wind farm on the Thames Estuary that will generate enough electricity to power 750,000 homes when finished.

Governments around the world must support the building of additions to the infrastructure that will allow the large-scale distribution of energy from renewable sources. Only then will these start-up businesses become profitable and thrive.

If your business and interests as an entrepreneur are not in the area of sustainable energy, then look instead at what your business can do to reduce emissions. Examine every aspect of your operation for ways that you can reduce, reuse and recycle. I assure you there are many! Changing your processes may not be easy, but, since the business sector has been partly responsible for creating the problem in the first place, we must also be part of the solution. At Virgin, all of our businesses are continually looking at how they can minimise the impact they have on the environment.

In the next ten years, we will all head into unknown territory as we face a vast increase in our demand for energy yet remain worryingly overdependent on oil. If entrepreneurs go into the field of renewable energy for the right reasons, along the way they are almost certain to create some very exciting new technologies and successful new businesses.

A lot of people are going to make a lot of money but, like the Klondike gold rush of the late 1800s, those who stake their claims first will be the ones to hit it big.

NEW VENTURES
Which to pick?

Q: How do you decide on new ventures and where to focus Virgin Group's attention?

– Isaac Polanco, Panama

A: *We didn't start out with a traditional master plan with sectors and new territories marked for expansion neatly mapped out. In fact, we still don't have that sort of plan or organisation, since we believe that our ongoing entrepreneurial, free-spirited flexibility is at the core of Virgin's success. This approach has had a profound impact on the way we develop our new businesses.*

At a casual glance, it might appear that we have been rather opportunistic in our choices over the years about the businesses and sectors into which we expanded. Initially, we moved into areas where I had a personal interest (such as music and media); then, as we began to understand more about Virgin's strengths in terms of customer service, it became industries that we felt were ready for a shake-up (airlines, health clubs, mobile phones); and, more recently, where my passion for exploration has taken us (space and deep-ocean tourism). Our choices were not random or merely reactive, but guided by our decision to take an entrepreneurial approach to expansion.

Instead of pushing our teams to do ever more intensive analysis to pick our next venture – aka 'paralysis by analysis', which inevitably slows the whole business down – I set a priority on our remaining open to new ideas. It is one of the reasons why I always urge people to pursue their own interests outside work and to take regular holidays. Exercising your creativity in other settings isn't just relaxing; you'll stay informed about developments in other fields and connect with a wider circle of people than you might encounter at work. Broadening your horizons keeps your thinking fresh and original and makes good business sense!

I had always loved music, for instance. In 1970, when Mike Oldfield pitched us his album Tubular Bells *after many record companies had turned him down, I recognised its value, as did my friends, and we decided to start up a company to help him find an audience. The album did so well that it helped establish Virgin Records and funded the launch of the company, which became the biggest independent record label in the world by the 1990s. Although we have sold our recording and retail businesses, Virgin still retains a connection to music through live music festivals.*

This brings me to my next point: you always have to be ready to capitalise on opportunities when they come along, and not be afraid to pounce. In the late nineties, established companies offering mobile phone services in Britain were finding it tough to attract the lucrative corporate market and the rapidly growing youth one. We took advantage of the opening by launching Virgin Mobile, which, using T-Mobile's physical plant and network, provided great service at a cheaper price and didn't require customers to lock into a complicated and expensive contract. We saw this as a classic opportunity to create a service orientated company aimed towards young people – as you could see from our cheeky marketing campaigns.

From this we learned the advantages of the Virgin-branded virtual network model, where we partner with an existing operator. Soon we rolled out similar businesses in the United States, Australia, Canada and France; we have since expanded into India and Latin America.

You must be fearless when venturing into new areas – assuming, of course, you have a clear understanding of what the risks are. The launch of our space-tourism business, Virgin Galactic, and our recent explorations of the ocean depths are great examples of this. We did not set ourselves these challenges on a whim, but only after years of working and exchanging ideas with experts in those fields. We are building on our technical experience in air travel and also our history of taking on difficult feats, such as our record-breaking balloon trips across the Pacific and

Atlantic, which required the acquisition of technical know-how in many different areas. You must heed the lessons of the past, but also be prepared to learn as you go: and, by comparison to many, I think it is fair to claim that at Virgin we are fast learners!

Finally, you need to seek out new opportunities, as well as react to those you encounter. At present, population growth and development are linked to increased consumption of natural resources and rising energy needs. Entrepreneurs who take time to inform themselves about the issues will spot opportunities to build new, sustainable businesses for present and future markets. We have set up the Virgin Green Fund to lead our effort and invest in the renewable sector. This is likely to be one of the biggest areas of investment in the next forty years; I hope that in the future Virgin becomes as well known for its activities in these areas as it is for music and aviation today.

There is no prescription for how best to build and expand your business or invest capital. Your choices should depend on your interests and goals, how a new company would fit with yours and on your tolerance for risk. Essentially you should learn to go with your instinct. It takes courage but over the years it has certainly served me well. Bon chance!

GET BIG

By staying small

Meeting with a group of small-business owners recently I was asked, 'How can we go about laying the foundation for a corporate culture like Virgin's?'

It's not a short answer but whether you're launching a new business or expanding an existing one, laying a solid foundation for the future is critically important – bringing in investors, getting your contracts right, hiring your core team members, choosing the right suppliers. The fact that you are thinking about this question shows that you already have a sense of where your priorities should lie and you're ready to follow through.

To be honest, when my friends and I started the first Virgin business forty years ago, we had no master plan – especially not one for a group of companies that by 2011 would number more than four hundred businesses around the world and employ 50,000 people. Had we tried to plan for such a future, we would certainly have messed it up.

If there is a 'right' way to develop your company's culture, our experience shows that it should evolve organically. In 1970, my friends and I weren't planning to do anything other than have a good time while doing something we loved that would hopefully be able to pay the bills. We loved listening to music, so we tried to sell records to other kids who wanted a fun place to hang out while deciding which ones to buy. We had no marketing plan or budget – our goals were simply to make enough money to pay the rent and our suppliers, and to have some cash left over at the end of the month.

Our launch was really no different from that of most small companies, since few entrepreneurs start thinking about their business's culture until it is already well established. If I think back to what we did right, it was in our planning process, when we made sure we were having fun working together and that everyone who had a good idea was included in our decision-making process. We had accidentally stumbled on the core elements of a culture dedicated to delivering great customer service! It turned out that people who work in a friendly environment that is tolerant of mistakes, and who are empowered to make decisions about how they do their jobs, arrive at the best possible solutions for serving customers.

When you're sorting out what your front-line colleagues' priorities should be, remember that how you treat the customer will form the basis of your corporate culture. Put your staff first, listen to them, and follow up on their ideas and suggestions.

Because you can be sure that every person on your staff

already has deep insights into what your customers want and what employees need in order to deliver it. Should they focus on delivering solutions tailored to each customer's needs? On building lasting customer relationships? Or should they quickly deliver the goods or services your company offers? Listen carefully and find ways to empower each person to do a great job. Sir Freddie Laker was famous for his standard response to any staffer who came to him to whine about something: 'Don't bring me problems, bring me solutions!' (He could certainly never be accused of running an autocracy.)

Small-business owners often find it tough to learn how to handle success. When a business does well, many owners/ chief executives start to focus solely on increasing profits, no matter what the cost – leaving behind everything that originally made the business special. The founder usually moves to a big corner office on the top floor and never again sets foot in the factory. Employees who were integral to the company's early success suddenly find they are the last to know what is happening, and their views are no longer valued or sought.

So try to ensure your company grows at a comfortable pace and, whenever possible, involve your employees in its evolution. If you are a small-business owner mulling over an expansion, tell all your employees about your plan – include everyone from the truck driver to your senior team – and ask for their input. If you can, it would be best to work out the details of the expansion plan together, taking into account the challenges faced by your employees, and incorporating improvements they would like to make. The ultimate winners will be your customers and the bottom line.

At Virgin, we have never had to struggle with the typical problems of big corporations, probably because we never really got big – we just diversified. Our growth was once described as 'vertical disintegration' because our new businesses frequently appear to be tangential or even completely unrelated to our core mission. When Virgin was known for producing and selling records, for instance, we started up an airline.

The traditional corporate response to our typical plan for a new business would be 'I'm sorry, but we're an XYZ company. That business is not within our core competency.' But we see a uniting factor in our dedication to customer service. Instead of becoming a huge, bloated entity locked into a single sector, these tangential forays have kept our company fresh and different – we are always learning new businesses and recruiting smart new people. Each Virgin company is run by its own largely autonomous management team that relies on the same small-business principles we've employed since the very beginning.

Whatever route you decide to take as you expand your business, make sure that it builds on your company's past successes, and that it fits with the corporate culture and the vision for the future that you and your team have created.

And when a critic says, 'That's not the way a big company would do it', take it as a huge compliment!

SELLING CUSTOMERS IS EASY

Selling investors is not

Okay, so you have this earth-shattering idea for a new business that you are convinced will create some serious waves, make mincemeat of the competition, and might just make you a fortune along the way.

You've checked and rechecked the competition, surveyed all your friends and family on it, drawn up a business plan and assembled a team – this is it – you're ready to take the leap.

Now comes the hard part.

Securing investment for a venture is a hurdle almost all entrepreneurs have to face, and most do it with extreme of trepidation. It involves spreading the word about your idea, finding prospective investors, and then defending your thesis – often with people with far more experience in the sector or, almost as bad, with idiots in suits who simply don't get it.

This is one of the most challenging stages for any entrepreneur. So much rides on these meetings – how to get it right? Unfortunately there is no 'one-size-fits-all' formula when preparing a pitch for potential investors, but here are a few tips that I have picked up over the years.

One of my first presentations did not go at all well. Investors had asked to see me about *Student* magazine, which my friends and I launched as teenagers. Flushed by our early success, I talked at (not with) our potential backers, stridently telling them about my ideas for extending the *Student* brand. It was going to take the world by storm going way beyond publishing to travel, hotels and music. I think they were terrified by this precocious youth … but one way or another they did not invest in our magazine.

Twenty years later, when I was trying to launch Virgin Atlantic Airways, I was much more attuned to my audience as I pitched the idea to my fellow directors at Virgin, and then to a Boeing executive. Though our group had no experience in the airline business, by then I had learned the valuable 'KISS' strategy: 'Keep it simple, stupid.' It is vitally important to present a clear, concise plan that investors can easily understand and repeat to their own people. In the first meeting avoid overly complicated, numbers-laden presentations. Sell them on the viability of the concept: you can fill in a lot of the nitty-gritty detail at the second meeting. I described our plan to steal market share from the established airlines with flights tailored to the needs of business-class passengers as well as offering an affordable service that would attract holidaymakers. Our focus on improving service, bringing fun and glamour back to air travel, and our record of success in the music industry must have impressed the Boeing executive as he soon agreed to lease us a used 747. And at that stage my somewhat wary colleagues became enthusiastic, too.

The most important difference between those two presentations was that in the second I put myself in my audience's shoes. Before you meet an investor, do some research: has the company ever made similar investments? Do they understand your sector or have experience with similar businesses. Tailoring your presentation to that person's knowledge of your industry sector will keep them interested.

Strict attention to detail is critical. Long before the day of the presentation, make sure you go over every claim, statistic and projection in your business plan, check them over thoroughly, then check them again and commit them to memory. Know the markets you are going to target, your competition and how you plan to make your mark, and be prepared to defend your argument. What are its weaknesses and how will we overcome them?

Before you pitch, do a practice run or three with trusted colleagues and advisers. Get each person to play devil's advocate and point out the warts you've been too close to see, or that haven't yet made it onto your radar. Tell them this is no-holds-barred time and that they aren't there to tell you what you want to hear, but rather what you need to know. Were your listeners persuaded? What did they find memorable? Could they repeat your message back to you? Take notes and act upon them – the next audience won't be so nice!

If you're preparing for a short meeting, pick three key points that will stick with potential investors. These should be things like: what makes your product or service different? Will it improve your customers' lives? Why would people buy it? Write these points down on a postcard-size piece of paper or even your shirt cuff, and make sure you keep your message focused. With luck, your potential backer will be intrigued enough to call you back for a second meeting.

Dress to make a good first impression. The success of companies like Google, Facebook and Twitter means that not every prospective investor expects – or would be impressed by – a suit and tie. However, being on time and comfortably well-dressed will help to build early rapport.

As you make your presentation, how you listen can be just as important as what you say. Pay attention to your audience's reactions and take the time to ask if they have questions. If it appears that you are not getting through, try to adapt your pitch to focus on the areas that interest them. And don't make the common mistake of speaking almost exclusively to the audience member who's nodding the most – he could be the one who's falling asleep!

If your proposal is rejected, it's not the end of the world. Ask for feedback. Did the investors really understand the idea? Do they have suggestions for improving your product or service? While their comments may be negative, it is important to keep in mind that their criticisms are not indicative of your chances of future success.

Finding investors to provide the capital you need for launch can be a long and often daunting process. So keep tweaking the pitch and move on to the next meeting.

Most of all, never forget that overcoming adversity is the mark of a true entrepreneur.

WHAT IS SUCCESS?

Some positive thoughts

Among the numerous email requests I receive for advice, a great many come from university students. They'll usually tell me they hope to become business leaders and entrepreneurs and seek guidance on everything from 'should I just take off and see the world?' to how to make the most money, to whether a career in business is right for them. The single most common theme, though, is 'success'. How did I get there? How can they be successful in their chosen field?

Rather than address the specifics of any one person's situation, however, let's look at the underlying question: what does 'success' really mean?

First, success in any career is closely tied to doing what you enjoy and developing your skills and talents. If you are considering a career as an entrepreneur, remember that leaders in this field are usually flexible and open-minded. They are able to imagine themselves in their customers' shoes. And they have empathy not only for their colleagues and employees but for the people who are affected by the business's operations. Business favours people who, when they see a problem or an injustice, try to do something about it. Does this describe you?

It can be difficult to assess one's own strengths and weaknesses. If you don't already have a mentor, it would be good to contact someone who has experience in the area you're thinking about entering. Professional organisations might be able to put you in touch with someone willing to help you review your best options.

Remember, a good mentor is not necessarily someone who is well known, but, rather, someone who is leading a rich and enriching life. Reach out to a business leader who has made a difference that is important to you.

At this stage, many young people are focused on developing abilities in areas where they haven't succeeded or exhibited much skill. Not long ago, I wrote to someone who, like me, is dyslexic. I said that it is important to try to excel at what you're good at. Don't let your limits knock your self-confidence. Put them to one side.

This is the time to focus on your strengths, because success as an entrepreneur is about ideas and excellence. Not excellence measured in awards, or other people's approval, but the sort one achieves for oneself by exploring what the world has to offer. So, rather than looking to others for your markers of achievement, consider what success means for you. Thinking about personal matters, like your hopes for your family and private life, might help you bring this vision into focus.

Are you dreaming about great wealth? Success in business has nothing to do with profits. Profits are necessary to invest in the next project – to pay the bills, repay investors and reward people for their hard work – but that's all. The reality is that, in business, money flows like a running stream. During one season, it might be a torrent, but then you have to invest in order to keep your business going, and your cash flow dries up overnight.

It seems like an American trait to talk about wealth. In Britain (and I have found in Canada, too) we're slightly embarrassed about it, and I think that's a good thing. When I go to a party I see people, not bank statements, and I'd like to think that others feel the same about me. Money is only interesting for what it lets you do and create.

If money is a poor guide to achievement, celebrity is worse. The media tends to personalise and simplify matters, and that's understandable. It's much easier for reporters to talk about Warren Buffett, Mark Zuckerberg, Bill Gates or even Richard Branson but that doesn't reflect the reality that a legion of senior people at those companies make many major decisions every day – they just don't talk to the media about it.

If neither money nor celebrity are fair measures of success, then what about personal power? Well, I have spent more than forty years building the Virgin brand, and if I were gone tomorrow our team would carry on without me, just as Apple will continue without Steve Jobs and Microsoft has carried on since Bill Gates stepped down as CEO in 2008.

Success in business is best measured by whether or not you have created something of which you can be truly proud – and whether or not you've made a real difference for others. This is what gets me up in the morning. It's why I've never wanted to run a big legacy company, and it's why I get huge enjoyment out of creating and tending to lots of smaller ones. Virgin, by remembering its roots as a small entrepreneurial company, has made a positive difference in many diverse fields, and for many people.

The more actively and practically engaged you are, the more successful you will feel. Right now, I find myself doing more and more to help safeguard our future on this planet. Does that make me successful? I don't know, but it certainly makes me happy.

When you are facing choices about your path to a career, and in all the choices that follow, focus on your own goals and try not to be distracted by those of others. Consider the needs of your community, and how you might best contribute. What is your vision for change? Start working towards that. In business, as in life, what matters is that you do something positive.

WHEN GOING WALKABOUT
Don't trip over your words

I have written earlier about the importance of senior executives going walkabout – or leaving their offices every now and then to take a stroll through their business, from the factory floor to the accounting department, to get to know their people better. But a friend recently took me to task: 'You're absolutely right, Richard, but frankly there are a lot of individuals who are better off being locked in their offices.'

He told me about a chief executive he'd once worked with who loved to go walkabout, but usually with disastrous results. It seemed that this CEO couldn't effectively express her appreciation for employees' efforts. Everywhere she went, she left behind a trail of discouraged workers because she was constantly guilty of 'damning with faint praise'. Like the Italians who used to declare 'At least Mussolini made the trains run on time', this CEO's half-hearted attempts at paying someone a compliment were so feeble that it would have been better if she'd said nothing at all.

Interestingly, families are adept at this particular art form. After a relative has slaved to put a really nice four-course dinner on the table, a teenager may say something like: 'Yum, that dessert was really great!' – the subtext of which is '... but the rest of it wasn't too good'.

Sometimes business leaders are similarly oblivious to just how damaging a poor turn of phrase can be. I recently heard the chairman of a multinational tell an audience, 'I am grateful for what our senior team has achieved over the last year'. I suspect that 'grateful for' was hardly an endorsement that sent them home feeling good about themselves. It should be abundantly clear to employees that their achievements are recognised and celebrated.

In the workplace, examples abound. Often, such miscommunications are about camouflaging bad news, but that doesn't help matters. I cringe when managers say things like, 'We didn't do badly', which doesn't mean they did well. Or, 'We did better than last year', when last year was a disaster. When the CEO I mentioned earlier was asked how things were going in her business, apparently her favourite response was 'It could be worse'.

Sometimes language itself can be a contributor to communication problems. In Virgin Records' early days, when a leading music industry executive from the US visited us in London, his conversations with us made us suspect that he was a bit disapproving about our artists and what we were doing at the label. It was only after a number of trips to the

United States that I worked out that he hadn't been at all negative – in fact, the opposite!

It came down to our differing interpretations of the word 'quite'. In British usage, if someone says, 'I think you have some quite good bands', it means you have some fair to middling performers. When an American says the same thing, he means that you have some very good bands.

No matter what the situation, as a business leader your job is to get your message across: to speak plainly and clearly. It is not easy, but it is necessary.

In many instances, it all comes down to paying attention to people's reactions. A CEO having trouble connecting with people as they go walkabout should take notice of their discomfort. In such situations, it is important to do more listening than talking. When a leader understands an employee's perspective, they will usually be able to find the right words with which to respond.

To address my friend's concerns about the potentially negative impact of going walkabout: I agree that it might not be the best thing to do if you're having a bad day. If that is the case, keep the door closed and your voice down. But if you must venture out, avoid statements like 'We're having an OK year'.

So, as my dad's favourite Bing Crosby record from the 1940s used to urge (play after play!), 'You've got to accentuate the positive/Eliminate the negative/Latch on to the affirmative/ And don't mess with Mister In-Between.'

If you pull it off, you will have done 'quite' well!

SURVIVING A DOWNTURN
And thriving
in the process

Having recently started out my seventh decade, I am old enough not to take a major recession lightly; on the other hand, having seen them before, I'm getting a feel for the market's cyclical upturns and downturns.

Each generation of politicians and economists tries to flatten the cycle of boom and bust, and every one of them fails to pull it off. So, I think it's time for a new approach: keep in mind that the economy has its ups and downs, and, by investing wisely, you can reduce the damage a downturn can do to your business or career.

Knowing what I know now, if I could go back to the beginning (and was interested solely in maximising my investments, which I'm not), I would invest only during recessions, when almost everything costs 50 to 90 per cent less than it does during boom times. This would be good for me as an investor, and the economy would benefit from the investment.

This is hard to do for two reasons, first because the economic cycle is slow – boom to bust can take a decade or more. We would have to learn patience. And the second reason is even more challenging: entrepreneurs have to respond to ideas as well as to the market.

There are times when an idea is ripe, but the market is wrong – a situation many entrepreneurs find themselves in right now. What should they do? Simply shrug their shoulders and walk away? Of course not: we can't just kill our entrepreneurial zeal with the touch of a button.

The answer is think big, but build small.

Create something you're proud of, but don't let it swallow you financially. You don't need to slather money over a good idea. A good idea will grow by itself. For years, private space programmes consisted of daring engineers in the middle of the desert attempting to launch one rocket after another. Today, thanks to aerospace engineer Burt Rutan's brilliance, the team at Virgin Galactic is working on the world's first feasible space tourism operation.

For all the misery the current recession has caused, you can be sure that fortunes are being made. There are big opportunities out there. Big homes that were worth five million are going for half that. Divide some big, handsome homes in university towns into good-quality student accommodation and – who knows? – you might soon be able to afford that big country house you always wanted. Which, by the way, is also now on offer for a fraction of its peak price.

The idea should be simple – simple enough for an individual

to turn it into a reality. Small, lean entrepreneurial companies are the future of business.

Not everyone is an entrepreneur. If you want to find out if you have what it takes, save your experiments for evenings and weekends. If you have a secure job, now is certainly not the time to hand in your notice unless you're absolutely certain that you have a brilliant idea. People on a salary will suffer relatively little during a downturn. Wages may well be frozen, or even reduced, but since the price of many things is coming down they will not be hurt much.

The prospects for people who lose their jobs are, of course, much worse.

If you are an employer, be aware that lay-offs are bad for business. The core of any company is its talent, its expertise and its relationships. Letting employees go must be a last resort. At the beginning of the downturn, we asked the chief executives in the Virgin Group to explore every avenue – from job sharing to reduced working weeks to wage freezes to unpaid leave – before they laid off staff.

And what if you've lost your job? Not long ago, a journalist asked me what my advice would be to the newly unemployed. I pointed out, as gently as I could, that there were many people better qualified than me to answer that question. But there is one thought I will share.

If a company had just let me go, I would look for ways for that very business to save money. All businesses – whether they're booming or busting, young or old, big or small – need to save money. If your office has an account with an expensive cab company, then find one that undercuts it. It burns regular light bulbs? As you take that slow walk to the lift, count the bulbs. Do the math. Show them the savings they could make by switching to energy-efficient bulbs, offer to make the arrangements and ask for a cut.

Many small entrepreneurial opportunities are there for the taking. Most have to do with saving energy. If there's one thing we know for sure, it's that fuel is going to get more expensive and probably sooner than later. Many companies have yet to understand that an ailing business can be boosted simply by reducing waste and using energy more efficiently. Most businesses have no idea how much money they're flushing away on unnecessary document printing, lights that stay on 24/7 for no reason, windows that could be cleaned half as often, energy-hungry office machinery, and pointless travel and shipment costs. Like when people say, 'I'll messenger it over right away' and it's something that doesn't even warrant the cost of a fax.

You worked there so you know the problems. You witnessed the waste for years as the money was burned but it was never in your remit to do anything that would take a cost-culture shift. Now's your chance to make a pitch – offer to do it for a percentage of the savings so they have nothing but upside.

Not every cloud has a silver lining but some of them most certainly do, and it takes a certain kind of rainmaker attitude to find which ones are which.

RISING ABOVE
IT ALL
Galactic adventures

Q: Why does space fascinate you so much?
– Iris Brueggler, editor, News.at (Austria)

A: *I have always tended to be adventurous. As a boy, I dreamed of becoming a professional sportsman but, after a knee injury ended that, I continued to explore the world through other means. While most people focus on my commercial ventures, I have also set records for crossing the Atlantic in a speedboat, hot-air balloon travel, both trans-Atlantic and trans-Pacific, and in 2004 set a record for the fastest amphibious vehicle crossing of the English Channel. Pursuing space exploration through Virgin Galactic is my latest and by far and away boldest adventure – one that poses interesting and complex technical challenges.*

Watching the final landing of space shuttle Atlantis *at Kennedy Space Center in Florida last month was a poignant moment for me. It marked the end of a journey that started when NASA's space shuttle programme was launched. Since then, those reusable vehicles have travelled 542 million miles and carried 355 people from sixteen different countries into space.*

Until now, the development of rockets, spaceships and space travel has been the purview of governments only: during the Cold War, winning the space race was a matter of national pride for the US and USSR. Now, with the end of the shuttle programme, the US government wants the private sector to develop the next generation of vehicles and platforms for near-space exploration and travel.

At Virgin Galactic, we are taking on that challenge, and plan to offer suborbital space travel from our base in New Mexico within the next two years. NASA's focus will now shift to designing and building a long-distance, multipurpose spaceship, Orion, *which they hope will be ready to transport humans to an asteroid by 2025 and to Mars by 2030. Long-distance and also a long way away!*

Q: Do you think man will ever be able to leave Earth and live on other planets?

A: *A few years ago, Virgin and Google planned a prank for April Fools' Day. On the day, I was giving a speech in Las Vegas. Towards the end I told my audience that I was going to give them a world exclusive: I announced the launch of a* *new venture called 'Virgle', with the aim of colonising Mars and building a city there.*

Providing few details, but with lots of enthusiasm, I explained how the Google founders, Larry Page, Sergey Bryn, and I were looking for volunteers ready to make the pioneering mission. Despite explaining that there would be no return ticket, eager adventurers swamped the stage, proving that many people still feel the excitement and hunger for exploration that accompanied our first steps into space. Even the requirement we posted that they 'must have an appreciation of algae as food' didn't seem to dampen anyone's enthusiasm!

While it may be a long time before a private company reaches and colonises other planets, government-funded missions are likely to reach Mars in our children's lifetime.

Q: You do a lot of charity activities, but today thousands of people are dying of hunger in Africa and other places. Wouldn't it be better to give all the money invested in your space venture to fight starvation?

A: *I believe we need to do both and they are in no way mutually exclusive. We do need to harness the power of government, NGOs and the business world to meet the challenges of famine, poverty and climate change that we face today, such as the recent appalling famine in Somalia. But this should not be at the cost of human endeavour: the exploration of space has a wider purpose as we look for clues about how to address climate change and minimise its effects.*

We will bring a fundamentally new market into space: the general public. When the first commercial flights were launched more than a hundred years ago (in Germany, by Zeppelin balloon); this accelerated the development of aviation technology, drove demand and, over time, lowered prices for the benefit of all. Orbital space travel will remain out of reach of the average citizen for some time, but suborbital space travel will be available to millions within the next decade.

Virgin Galactic's architecture may help us to move beyond the jet-travel plateau of the last fifty years, providing the basis for the evolution of point-to-point transportation on Earth. Someday, an innovation in suborbital travel could dramatically reduce the time it takes to move about the globe. We should be able to develop space planes that can travel from London to Sydney in just a few hours.

Our space programme is designed to be as forward thinking as possible: our vehicles are almost completely reusable, which is the most important innovation required for radically lower-cost space transportation. And beyond our initial plans for space tourism, I hope we will use Galactic's technology to develop commercial operations for launching small satellites and conducting scientific research in space.

Space exploration is essential to humanity's future wellbeing. As government agencies refocus their efforts, our picking up the baton and embarking on the adventure of developing safe, clean and commercially viable technologies for space travel is a terrific challenge, and one that will make a difference to the planet. One thing's for sure: the sky is no longer the limit!

LIVING THE BRANSON LIFE
The view from my hammock

People often ask me what drives me – what motivates me to continually pursue new challenges. They also like to know how I got to where I am today and how I like to spend my time away from work. Here is a glimpse into my life and some possible tips for yours.

What motivates me?

What has been described as an almost childlike curiosity for learning about new things, trying new ventures and meeting new people. I have been very fortunate to have led an interesting life. Part of that has been because of my willingness – and all the great people at Virgin's willingness – to keep trying new and sometimes borderline-crazy ventures.

How important to me is money?

I pursue only those things about which I can be passionate, whether that will make money or not. I find that if you are really fervent and committed, you can only do better – and have a better chance of making the venture pay the bills. Money has enabled me to start up and support a number of philanthropic causes through Virgin Unite. I hope we can play a part in leaving the world in better shape than we found it.

Whom do I admire personally and professionally?

One of the best things about my life is getting to meet many incredible people on my travels and through the company. We now employ 50,000 people worldwide and, as often as I can, I pop into the offices to meet and talk with the staff. Not only do they all give 150 per cent and really believe in what they are doing – which helps keep me going – but they're also great fun and love a party, which keeps me young. Well, young at heart, anyway!

Outside of my friends, family and staff, here are a few of the people I admire: I have already mentioned the influence of the late Sir Freddie Laker, the founder of Laker Airways, the first 'no frills' carrier who was a wise and gracious mentor to me when I entered the world of aviation; Nelson Mandela, the anti-apartheid activist who spent twenty-seven years in prison before he became president of South Africa; Desmond Tutu, the first black South African Anglican Archbishop of Cape Town, South Africa, who chaired his country's Truth and Reconciliation Committee; Peter Gabriel, the successful English musician and songwriter (once the lead vocalist and flautist for the rock band Genesis), who now is an inspired producer and promoter of world music and humanitarian causes; the late Mo Mowlam, who was the Secretary of State for Northern Ireland when the historic Good Friday Peace Agreement was signed in 1998; and the aviation genius Burt Rutan, an American aerospace engineer who designed Voyager, the first plane to fly around the world without stopping or refuelling, and the sub-orbital space plane SpaceShipOne, the first privately funded spacecraft to enter the realm of space twice within a two-week period.

Every one of them has exhibited incredible courage, talent and a zest for getting things done no matter how long the odds, a trait that I really admire.

Who or what inspires me in life?

I have had great support from my family and friends. Two very different characters spring to mind. First is the late Steve Fossett, a dear friend and fellow adventurer. We first met when we were competing for ballooning records. In the end we combined our efforts, and Steve flew non-stop around the world in the Virgin Atlantic Global Flyer, on a single tank of fuel. He also climbed the Matterhorn and Mount Kilimanjaro, he swam the English Channel, was placed forty-seventh in the Iditarod dog sled race and participated in the 24 Hours of Le Mans car race. Steve kept on pushing and challenging himself, taking on the seemingly impossible and often achieving it. Before he tragically died in a still unexplained plane crash, Steve had probably checked off 90 per cent of the adventures on his 'bucket list'. Truly a real life superhero!

Nelson Mandela`s highly documented life and story has inspired me tremendously. He went through many hardships with unfailing dignity and strength and has devoted his life to making his country and our world a better place. Recently, we worked together with Peter Gabriel to set up the Elders, a group of former world leaders who are using their wisdom and experience to resolve world conflicts. It is fascinating – in fact downright extraordinary – to listen to this group of eminent global leaders and to see what they are trying to do to mitigate the causes of human suffering. Next time you're online, check it out at www.theelders.org.

How does a typical day in my life look?

I don't think I have many days that could be described as 'typical'! A day at home on Necker Island is probably about as close as it gets. It really is the perfect place for work, play and life. I always wake early – I love that quiet time in the morning. Let's face it: I have the most beautiful office in the world – a hammock overlooking the British Virgin Islands! A fantastic place for reflection, it sets me up for the day and the surprises that are bound to happen. I come up with more ideas in that hammock than I ever would sitting in a glassed-in cage ... Sorry, I meant to say 'an office'. Plus Necker is well positioned to deal with all the time zones in which Virgin operates. At least, that's my excuse and I'm sticking to it!

I like to start my day with a swim then after breakfast I hit the phone. I still far prefer talking to people to having email relationships. I don't have set start and finish times. At the end

of the day, I like to play tennis to unwind, then grab a drink as
the sun goes down.

How do I relax?

I know some of you are thinking that 'typical' day sounds
pretty relaxing but, since I travel the majority of the time,
there's nothing better than heading home to spend time with
my family and friends. I love to surf or go kite surfing with my
son, Sam, and my nephews, play a game of tennis with friends
or sail around the islands. These are all good ways to unwind.
I love to be 100 per cent fit and healthy and love to find ways
to achieve that. There is really nothing more important. You
must find time for yourself and your body.

How do I spoil myself? Any guilty pleasures?

Pretty boring really; I enjoy the occasional bar of chocolate
– or one of my wife Joan's amazing fried egg sandwiches!
OK – and I do enjoy a party.

EARLY ENDEAVOURS
Can pay dividends later in life

Now that my own children have grown up and are striking out on their own in business, I love receiving questions like this one from Texas.

> **Q:** My twelve-year-old has often tried to launch little businesses, but he becomes frustrated when he fails. He tried making and selling wallets, then selling his artwork. He also set up a lawn-mowing service, but Mom and Dad were his only customers.
>
> I want him to continue to pursue his ideas, but I don't know how to help him succeed. Any suggestions?
> *– Debbie Mitchell, USA*

> **A:** *First of all, your son shouldn't be disheartened – with all his restless activity, he is off to a good start. Indeed, he has achieved the first step, which is just to turn up and try. And he is showing good instincts. One of my golden rules for the Virgin Group is that any business we decide to launch*

should enhance customers' lives. His lawn-mowing service certainly passes the test.

Tell him not to be discouraged. Any good entrepreneur must take risks when starting new ventures, and most enterprises do not work the first time around. Now he needs to take the second step, which is to learn from his mistakes and ensure he doesn't repeat them next time.

My own initial schoolboy attempts at setting up businesses were remarkably similar to your son's. As a teenager I tried my hand at all kinds of ventures, hoping to earn money. Two stand out, but sadly because of the suddenness of their demise.

When I was thirteen years old, I tried to grow Christmas trees in a field near our home in Sussex. I did it with the help of my best friend, Nik Powell, who would later become my business partner. We thought the trees would grow quickly and so be ready for harvest four years later. Over the Easter holidays we dutifully planted four hundred seedlings, then went back to boarding school and waited for our fortune to grow. We had worked out that when the trees grew to six feet tall, we could sell them for £2 each, generating £800 in profit from our initial £5 in seed capital (sorry, I couldn't resist it!). But when we returned home that summer, we found that the local rabbits had feasted on all the saplings and our plans were ruined.

My next venture involved breeding budgerigars, as I knew that they bred quickly; also, unlike the trees, I could sell them year round, rather than just before Christmas.

I calculated how much they would cost to buy, what their food cost and how much I could sell them for, then persuaded my father to build a huge aviary. The birds multiplied rapidly, and soon everyone in the village had at least two.

I returned to school after the summer holidays, leaving my long-suffering parents with the task of tending to my rapidly expanding inventory of birds. One day I received a letter from my mother saying that, tragically, rats had somehow got into the cage and eaten all my birds: I was heartbroken. It was many years later that Mum confessed to having been so fed up with cleaning out the enormous cage that she had deliberately left the door open.

Those stories may be comical now, but, looking back, it's clear I did learn a lot from those experiences. When I started up Student *magazine at age fifteen, I was much better versed in which pitfalls to look out for. Neither rats nor rabbits were ever a problem for the magazine!*

So it is important that your son keep trying. He is on the right track with the lawn-mowing business. It is a service many people want and should be happy to pay for.

Together, the two of you should take a second look at a few key factors and see if a tweak or two might kick-start Mitchell's Gardening Services:

1. Is the pricing right?

Are you charging too much? What do other kids charge? If you are unsure what to charge, you might try the radical

*approach: offer to mow people's lawns for free and tell
them that if they are happy with your work, they can pay
whatever amount they think is appropriate. You never
know – you may end up making more money than you
expected.*

2. Is the equipment up to date?

*Maybe you need to invest in a better lawnmower to
help your son woo customers – perhaps people in your
neighbourhood want the option of composting the
clippings? It is amazing how a loan from one's family will
focus an entrepreneur's mind.*

3. Do some research to find your most likely customers

*If old Mr Smith next door has just hurt his knee he might
love to have someone do his mowing. Are there other
people nearby who might need extra help, for any reason?
A young couple with a new baby, or someone about to go
on holiday?*

4. Can you broaden the services you offer?

*Some people like to mow lawns themselves – could you
also offer to weed gardens, clean cars or remove rubbish?
If your son demonstrates that he is reliable and works hard,
people may sign up for more than one service.*

5. Offer to donate some of your proceeds to a local charity

That may help you persuade people to try out your services, since you will also be doing some good for the community.

Finally, don't forget to look for some element of fun to sell your services. Laugh a lot, tell a few jokes and, above all, smile while you work. It is amazing what you can achieve with a little humour.

Maybe a slogan like, 'Mitchell's – Mower Value for Your Money'. Or maybe not!

CHANGE IS GOOD

As long as it is managed

Restructuring is a difficult process, right? Even if you've done everything right, sometimes you have to take your company in a new direction because circumstances and opportunities have changed. Companies aren't future-proof – no company lasts for ever.

Over the years at Virgin we have closed down or sold quite a few of the six hundred or so companies we have created – something our critics regularly point out. But what's wrong with that? Our strategy has often been to build a business up and once it's successful, sell a stake to release funds to start a number of new ones. Companies are tools, each designed to fulfil a particular purpose. If they are superseded or no longer needed, we will sell them or shut them down. We try our level best not to lose any people or know-how, but we don't allow ourselves to get nostalgic about the company itself. When Virgin renews itself, the critics who tut-tut about all the leaves falling to the ground have usually taken their eyes off the tree itself.

If you plan to lead your company through a restructuring, first you need to take a cold, hard look at the business. Are you really going to be able to empower your staff to do the job that needs to be done? It can be superhumanly difficult to change a company's existing culture. This is also something you should consider if you're leading a team that's contemplating a business acquisition – so many of which end up being disasters because the executives involved fail to understand the many challenges of getting different types of employees to work together and share the same goals.

We found ourselves grappling with a challenging situation in 2007, when we relaunched the combined company of NTL, Telewest and Virgin Mobile as Virgin Media, creating the largest Virgin company in the world, with ten million customers and 13,000 UK employees.

Until then I'd always followed a 'small is beautiful' business plan. Keeping the businesses small and intimate was easy to do in the record business where we would regularly spin off (pun intended) new labels whenever one of the existing rosters was getting too big. But this time around Virgin Media was neither small nor beautiful. The NTL part of our business, in particular, was in a very sorry state. We needed to make drastic changes in the area of customer service where the people dealing with (too numerous) complaints appeared totally unmotivated and uninterested. We soon found out why: they were reading from scripts all day!

This brings me to my next bit of advice: management overseeing any restructuring or merger should find ways to inspire all employees to think like entrepreneurs. Whatever you do, treat them like adults. A person's own conscience is usually the hardest taskmaster of all, so the more responsibility you give people, the better they will perform.

So, in Virgin Media's case, the offending scripts went straight into the rubbish bin. We told our call-centre employees to solve problems within one call if possible, and we reallocated resources to the front line to fix the problems at source.

There was scepticism at first among former NTL staff. What would happen if one of our customer service people overstepped the mark? What if they started offering customers too many perks? Our response to that was 'live and learn'. I didn't think anyone should be criticised for being overly generous when handling a disgruntled customer. If one or two of our people got themselves into a tangle, it just meant that they'd do better next time. And Virgin Media went on to become the UK's leading provider of cable TV, Internet and phone services.

The lesson I have learned from this and other, even more difficult restructurings is: avoid taking on someone else's legacy. If the people no longer have the enthusiasm and determination needed to relaunch the company, you are better off finding a new team or you may be better off starting from scratch.

But what if moving on is not a viable option? There is an alternative, one of the hardest tricks in the book: restructure your company so that it's very small, very specialised and very expensive. Turn it into a 'boutique' operation. This is an innovation of the highest calibre. Take a large operation and find ways to scale it down, retarget it and remarket it, all the while adding value that justifies the hike in price. It's tough to do, not least because you're in so much pain as you're doing it.

Why go down this route? If you're able to pull off the small-and-specialised restructuring, your staff may be in charge of a smaller company, but each contributor will have more clout and be much more focused. They will be able to take pride in their successes, and learn quickly and well from their failures.

What's more, you'll be gathering people together in a way that will have them bouncing ideas off each other, befriending and taking care of each other, and eventually they'll start coming to you with solutions and great ideas again.

Wouldn't it be wonderful if the company you recreate were full of motivated, caring, creative people? Think of what you could achieve, then take a very deep breath.

MANAGING THE LAUNCH

When the tough get going

Q: As much as I agree with you and think of you as a role model, I find some of your recommendations rather unrealistic, especially for businesses just starting up.

I would like to keep my employees happy but find it a great challenge due to limited resources. I'm unable to pay my employees well, as my priority is to make money and turn this business into a reality. On the other hand, my employees want good salaries and to work in a slick environment.

All these conflicting priorities force me to micro-manage my staff to get results. Please advise what I should do to make my employees happy.

— *Emily Bosco, Kenya*

A: *Emily brings up an interesting and challenging dilemma for entrepreneurs: during a business's precarious launch stage, can one truly afford to be generous, foster an atmosphere* *of fun and caring and give employees freedom?*

It is not only realistic, but vital to your new business's long-term success.

When I look back at our early days at Student *magazine, I had hardly any money to pay my staff or improve our premises. In fact, we worked in a basement flat, with the furniture limited to a few beanbags and some desks and phones. But the thrill and promise of possible success united us and ensured that we all worked long hours in cramped conditions. Despite the low pay, no one complained – everyone was intent on making the magazine work.*

The same was true of our first Virgin companies – a mail-order business selling records, and later, a few record stores. Again, we tried to keep the vibe relaxed, maintaining small, uncomplicated and friendly offices. This decision paid off, attracting great team members who were drawn by the flexible working conditions, and the fact we were all having fun doing it.

We always tried to create an atmosphere of team spirit and mutual appreciation. At Student, *we had a party or at least a few drinks whenever a staffer brought in an important new advertising account, and we celebrated the publication of every edition. We tried to make sure everyone had a great time at work, which generated great loyalty.*

My philosophy has not changed since then: do something you enjoy and your enthusiasm will rub off on others, ensuring that you have a committed and spirited team. In fact, for more than forty years I have felt that one of my most important jobs is to attract and motivate great people who genuinely seem to feel that their job is more important than just money.

Emily's concerns about micromanaging her team are valid. Employees will not take responsibility for their own actions if they feel the boss is looking over their shoulders all the time. They will not take the initiative to work that extra hour, make that extra call or squeeze that little bit more out of a negotiation.

The credit for Virgin's enduring and varied success is often attributed to me, but it's actually due to the people who piloted those businesses and the employees themselves. My biggest contribution has always been my willingness to give our people autonomy, responsibility and encouragement to take risks and just get it done.

And when our music business was becoming too big and top-heavy in terms of management, we split it in two, to ensure everyone focused on music and not internal politics. We kept doing this until we had nine or ten companies each in its own building. This helped us sign great acts during the seventies and eighties, such as the Sex Pistols and Culture Club.

When things do go wrong, you must teach yourself to listen to your employees and encourage them to find solutions. If you're worried by the business's finances, share this with your team and then listen to their suggestions for improving the situation. Your employees should never feel like hired hands, but fellow entrepreneurs.

Finally, it sounds as though some employees are not working out at Emily's business. If you find yourself in this situation, take a long, hard look at yourself and how you are treating your employees. Then look at your senior team (the rot starts at the top) to determine if they are effective team leaders. Letting people go should be your very last lever but if you have someone who is de-motivating the team, you may well have to bite the bullet.

Managers should never rule by fear. I find enthusiasm, genuine openness and camaraderie with your people are far better. Successful entrepreneurs usually have excellent people skills that exponentially increase their ability to make things happen.

So remember: encourage, enthuse, try to make work fun. Practise these skills at your small business; work on them every day. If you do, perhaps you will someday have the opportunity to continue practising – at your large business!

A SHOCKING REVELATION!

Even CEOs make mistakes

Okay, I admit it – I am not always right. There, I said it – in print no less! That just won me several bets.

Seriously, however, I can admit this without embarrassment, because it is true of all business leaders and entrepreneurs. It can be a difficult thing for an executive or manager to acknowledge to employees but errors of judgement (aka mistakes) do happen and anyone who accepts a leadership position should be prepared to own up to them.

As a leader, your decisions will be carried out, but that doesn't mean they will always be the best ones – or that changing circumstances can't turn a good call into a bad one overnight.

As years go, 2003 wasn't exactly a vintage year for our group. Around the time Apple introduced its iPod personal music player in 2001, a couple of very bright people from

Palm sold me on their own funky version of the MP3 player and a range of accessories. Virgin's management team strongly argued the financial analysis did not stack up and that we would have to sell a very high number of units to make it work. I insisted we push on and launch our very own MP3 player, Virgin Pulse! I felt the product fitted well with our brand, our music business and our heritage. And I suppose I wanted to turn my original April Fool's joke into a reality.

We spent $20 million designing our MP3 player and bringing it to market. Though that product and its successors were critically acclaimed in the United States, the Virgin Pulse bombed and we had to write off our investment.

Why didn't our product work? Because, simply stated, Apple had a brilliant and unbeatable strategy.

For Apple 2003 was notable because it launched its iTunes store that year – as the company simultaneously pushed down iPod prices very quickly. If a company drives down the retail price of an innovative new product fast enough when it is still the dominant player in the new market, no one else can catch up because they can't make enough money from their new products. When Apple introduced the cheaper, smaller iPod 'nano', it slammed the door on anyone else trying to build a significant market share in the digital music business. And, yes, I did freely admit that I was wrong; which helped us beat a hasty retreat from the marketplace before we lost even more money.

It can be very hard to own up to your mistakes when a big investment is not salvageable – and especially when it is a cause you alone have championed. This fear of embarrassment prevents many chairmen and senior executives from doing their jobs properly and addressing the situation when it is most urgent. If the business is disappearing, you must face your team and start looking into what is going on – and the sooner the better. Only by leaving the safety of your office and sampling the product or service yourself, studying the competition's offerings and generally turning your operation upside down will you get to the bottom of where and why things have gone awry.

When you have uncovered the problem, get the right people working on fixing it. In this situation, honesty is the only policy. If you speak openly and bluntly about why you had hoped a strategy would work, why this proved to be wrong, and how you and your team arrived at the solution you want to put in place, then your people will be better able to implement it. This is not the time to hold back information or delegate the blame. This may be one of the more difficult moments of your career, but you will not lose people's trust and respect by taking responsibility for the problem and admitting to your mistakes. People look for leaders to make informed decisions, not to be infallible.

If you discover that the problem was in the implementation of a service or product, do not make the beginner's mistake of firing those responsible. Blame and recriminations may offer a spiteful form of short-term comfort, but they will be toxic to your company and will stunt your recovery or the launch of future enterprises. It's unlikely that you will even need to talk to those employees about where they went wrong; if you provide all the information necessary, they will know what they did and be very eager to prove that they can get it right. If you keep your team together, you will close the door on rivals who might benefit from your mistakes by hiring the very people who have just learned the lesson the hard way.

Real innovation is about change – and when your plans to introduce a new product or service don't work out, sometimes you have to adapt to changing circumstances instead of forcing your competitors to play catch-up. As I've written before: get over it and move on. If that means taking a hit, then take it on the chin. Don't even think about it again. Just move forward.

But come on now: let's be fair about the Virgin Pulse. This wasn't just any old competitive response – it was the iPod! I mean, how was I supposed to know?

A NOOSE AROUND THE NECK
Ties that don't bind

While out walking in London recently, I passed a group of uniformed schoolchildren moving in an orderly, single-file line, with teachers in front and rear.

Nothing unusual, except for one thing that made me laugh out loud: their identical school ties. Or more accurately, what was left of them. More than half of the kids had cut their ties so that only three or four inches remained below the knot.

Intrigued, I asked the teacher who was bringing up the rear, 'So what happened to the ties?'

He chuckled and said, 'Well, the kids hate wearing them, but school rules say they have to. What the rules fail to specify, however, is how long they have to be – so, snip-snip!'

Why didn't I come up with such a naughtily innovative solution when I went to school?

This caught my eye because Virgin just got into the banking business with the acquisition of Northern Rock, a British bank that we are gradually rebranding Virgin Money. In British banking, few things strike terror in the heart of a customer quite as much as the prospect of facing a tie-wearing, three-piece-suited bank manager across a huge mahogany desk. So we redesigned the banks.

One of our first changes was to remove the traditional wooden counters and replace them with informal seating areas. We also thought that the staff's formal business attire was almost as solid a barrier to customer-friendly experiences as those counters were. When (to applause no less) we told our newest group of Virgin employees that (within reason) they could now wear whatever they want, the ties were the first thing to go.

I don't use the word 'hate' often but I have always hated ties. Maybe because I've never seen the point. They are uncomfortable and serve no useful purpose. I am lucky to have always worked for myself, and therefore have never been a victim of corporate dress codes. For years, a sweater and jeans were my standard business attire. Someone once joked, 'The day Richard shows up at the bank wearing a suit and tie, you'll know that we are in serious trouble.'

Lately I have actually taken to wearing a jacket, which is handy since I encounter many different climates and situations through my business travel, but I will only wear a tie under extreme duress, which usually means some boring club that won't let me in without a tie!

Suits and ties in an office are just another type of uniform, but in an arena where uniforms no longer serve any useful purpose. At one time they probably showed that the wearer was, at the very least, able to purchase and maintain a fairly expensive piece of fabric. Now, however, in an individualised, interconnected culture, your achievements speak for themselves. The suit and tie is an anachronism.

It used to be that the one male in the room with an open neck (which was usually me) would be self-conscious about it (which wasn't me). Nowadays, however, I am delighted to note that it's the man wearing the tie who is most likely to be the odd person out.

Probably one of the biggest breakthroughs in the gradual demise of the suit-and-tie dress code came, rather surprisingly, in some lofty political circles. Tony Blair was one of the first British prime ministers – Maggie Thatcher excepted – to frequently appear in public without 'proper' neckwear (to the outrage of the *Daily Mail*). Now President Obama has carried it to a level where he seems to be tieless almost 50 per cent of the time.

I have always prided myself on throwing out the rulebook when something proves a barrier to business – or is just plain silly. And there is no viable argument why 'gentlemen' should wear ties. The best anyone can muster is usually: 'It's expected,' or 'Everyone else will be wearing one.' One of the signs that business culture has changed is that when people arrive for a business meeting with me, invariably the first thing they ask is, 'Do you mind if we remove our ties?' They surely never thought, 'If we don't wear our ties we'll stand a lesser chance of getting the deal done.' So why did they wear them in the first place?

So on behalf of the oppressed tie-wearers of the world, here is my appeal to those corporate despots who still force their male employees to put nooses around their necks every day: Please think again.

TODAY'S FAILURE

Can lead to tomorrow's success

Recognising failure and recovering from mistakes are essential skills for any entrepreneur. When I recently received several excellent questions from readers of *Entrepreneur* magazine and American Express Open Forum, it prompted me to reflect on how I've dealt with missteps in my own career.

> **Q: I've been an entrepreneur for four years now and would like to know, when a business is not going well, how to tell when it's time to call it quits and switch to something else? You have mentioned your financial difficulties at the beginning of your career and as Virgin ventured into all kinds of media businesses. What helped you decide whether you wanted to stick it out or change sails?**
>
> **– Victor Tan, USA**

> **A:** *The impending failure of a business is something that you will instinctively recognise deep down, but human nature*

may put blinkers on that prevent you from acknowledging it. Most start-ups are short of cash in the launch stages and then lurch from one crisis to another as they struggle to keep afloat. In such situations, entrepreneurs need to be strong-willed, confident without being cocky, and determined to make an idea work, often against odds that may seem overwhelming.

I have lost count of the number of times rivals, reporters, bankers and even my own finance directors have told me that our time was up – but almost every time I kept going and tried another angle, convinced that our situation was not as dire as it appeared. We have sold houses, hotels and even other major businesses to raise cash. Sometimes we expanded our way out of trouble by ordering new planes, signing new bands or even buying new nightclubs.

However, you must balance this dogged streak with a sense of realism. There will be times when you must accept that, despite your best efforts, an idea or business cannot be saved. As they say, the first cut is the kindest – both to the venture being set loose and to the parent company. Overall, it seems to me that if you have been struggling to pay the bills and salaries on a regular basis; if you cannot get traction with customers; if you can't raise awareness of your product or brand, then it is time to quit.

Some of the best decisions our team at Virgin has made involved exiting markets early, when we could see that our product, service or brand was not making a big enough impression on customers, and would not break through and attract volume sales.

I also must confess that on occasion we've kept businesses afloat too long. Another venture impacted by the rise of MP3 downloading was Virgin Megastores. With new technologies stifling CD sales and retailers folding around the world, the business was losing a lot of money. We did not make a speedy exit in part because I resisted closing the business. I was worried about losing the flagship stores' presence in Times Square and on Oxford Street since they were so important to brand recognition and such a huge link with the past. But the scale of the losses meant that we had to sell the business to its management and focus our attention on markets where we could be the disruptor, not the disrupted.

Q: How do you regroup when disappointment is overwhelming? Do you have a three-day funeral and then get on with designing a new venture?

– Doug Warren, USA

A: *My mother drummed into me from an early age that I should not spend much time crying over spilt milk. I have always tried to bring that discipline to my business career. Over the years, my team and I have tried our best never to let mistakes, failures or mishaps get us down. Instead, even when a venture has failed, we seek out new opportunities to see whether we can capitalise on another gap in the market.*

Consider our much-publicised attempt to buy the failing British bank Northern Rock in 2009. After months of hard work, Virgin Money had put together what we considered to be a strong consortium in order to buy the bank and refinance its debts. Then Prime Minister Gordon Brown's government thought otherwise and nationalised the bank.

I was astounded. I spent a night drowning my sorrows with a few friends on Necker Island but by the time the hangover wore off we were hard at work mapping out how we would set up our own bank and then take on Britain's largest financial institutions. In late 2011 we were given the opportunity to bid for the then nationalised Northern Rock and I'm pleased to say that this time we succeeded. Our hard work paid off and we are now busy rebranding it as Virgin Money. Persistence pays!

REAL CHANGE FOR GOOD?

Entrepreneurs must take the lead

As we advance into the second decade of the twenty-first century, gloomy financial news from Europe and the United States, protests on Wall Street, in London and around the world, and the near-collapse of several European economies has understandably led many people to question the way we do business. They believe that our society has lost its way, encouraging greed and short-term thinking at the expense of investments in our future.

We should not lose sight of the fact that capitalism has improved our world by creating jobs, spurring innovation and lifting many people out of poverty. However, as the global population increases, so does demand for goods and services, which further depletes the planet's natural resources. At the same time, economic inequality is on the rise.

Business as usual is no longer an option. People all over the world are realising that we must find a way to harness the power of the free market in ways that directly address concerns for our society and the planet.

The good news is that this is a great opportunity. Business can change the world – it can be a genuine force for good. There are many great examples out there today. Some of these are profit-making, such as Participant Media, a company devoted to making movies that entertain and inspire the world, and Barefoot Power, an enterprise that has reportedly brought electricity to a million people for the first time through solar power. Rather than providing profits for shareholders, some such companies put their earnings back into growing their enterprises. Consider the Big Issue, a UK magazine publisher that provides work for homeless people, and the Khan Academy, which uses online learning tools to transform mathematics education all over the world.

At Virgin, our efforts arose from our connection with customers and our focus on customer service, as we began to try to combine the creation of profitable companies with support for our community and the environment. The second Virgin enterprise we ever launched, after the mail-order record company, was a student advisory centre that provided information on sexual health issues. (Later, in 1987, we set up Mates Condoms as part of our work to help combat the spread of AIDS.)

Such efforts can be found across the Virgin Group and, seven years ago, we established our own non-profit foundation, Virgin Unite, to help harness that entrepreneurial energy. Unite works with all of our businesses to help them to focus on driving positive change. More recently, Virgin Money founded Virgin Money Giving, an online donations hub that has generated more than £65 million for charities in the United Kingdom. In the United States, Virgin Mobile has reached out to customers and the public for help with the fight to end youth homelessness. This campaign has already positively impacted the lives of more than 35,000 young people.

Virgin Unite also brings together partners to launch independent initiatives focused on new approaches to global leadership, such as the Carbon War Room, which works to deliver market-driven solutions to climate change. One breakthrough of the Carbon War Room is it has unlocked around $650 million of investment into energy efficiency retrofits in Florida and California, which should eventually create more than 17,000 jobs.

We call this new approach to commerce 'Capitalism 24902', and we are now focused on getting business leaders around the world (24,902 miles in circumference) to look at how we can all do what's right for people and the planet. It's not really a case of choosing social good over profits; it's about social and environmental good becoming the driving forces of capitalism.

Many new businesses are embedding these core values from the start, but we are also seeing lots of existing businesses overhaul their operations and reap the benefits. Interface Global, the carpet manufacturer, is a good example of how this new approach can work. In an industry where companies typically have a large and toxic environmental impact, Interface

Global has transformed the way it sources raw materials, makes carpets and disposes of its waste – and it has created a more profitable business.

Other success stories: in the UK Marks & Spencer launched 'Plan A' in 2007, and, as a result, the company reports that it now recycles 94 per cent of the waste generated by its stores, has reduced carbon emissions by 13 per cent and in 2010 saved more than £70 million (over $100 million). General Electric launched 'Ecomagination' to create new products and services that help solve energy, efficiency and water challenges. GE invested $5 billion in research and development over five years and say they have generated more than $70 billion in revenues. As entrepreneurs and business leaders, we can follow their lead and realise the benefits.

How is your company uniquely positioned to contribute to your community? For ideas, listen to, learn from and empower everyone in your company to do what is right for people and the planet. Capitalism 24902 is all about people. Give your team the chance to make a difference, and they will tackle the project with enthusiasm and true engagement.

My most recent book, *Screw Business as Usual*, is all about celebrating the stories of people who have already shown that business can be a force for good. I am already looking forward to writing the sequel with a whole new list of stories about companies that have latched on to the fact that doing good is good for the community as well as for business.

I hope that yours will be one of them!

BE A LEADER
Not a boss

There used to be a school of parenting whereby children were supposed to be 'seen and not heard'. Countless generations of kids grew up in homes where the only justification a parent would ever have to offer for just about anything was 'Because I say so!'

Not surprisingly this carried forward into classrooms and workplaces where teachers and bosses simply replaced the parent as authority figures whose word was law.

Fortunately I grew up in a household where healthy debate was a way of life and, although my mother Eve usually had the last word (and still does), my sisters and I were encouraged to express our thoughts on anything and everything.

School was a different story, however, and my combination of dyslexia and rebelliousness should have made it abundantly clear to even the most casual observer that I was never destined to be anything but my own boss. Or, as my headmaster at Stowe School once put it, 'By twenty-one,

Branson, you'll either be a millionaire or in prison.'

As it turned out, from the day I dropped out of school I have always been lucky enough to be my own boss and have never ended up behind bars – well, maybe once, but very briefly!

Perhaps, therefore, it is odd that if there is any one phrase that is guaranteed to set me off it's when someone says to me, 'Okay, fine. You're the boss!' What irks me is that in 90 per cent of such instances what that person is really saying is 'Okay, then, I don't agree with you but I'll roll over and do it because you're telling me to. But if it doesn't work out I'll be the first to remind everyone that it wasn't my idea.'

In today's business world I see this classic image of 'the boss' as a total anachronism. It may work in certain connotations like 'organised crime boss', 'union boss' or 'pit boss', but being bossy per se is not an attribute that I have ever seen as desirable in a manager or anyone else for that matter.

Some might say this is only a matter of semantics, but I truly believe that forward thinking workplaces benefit from a pronounced absence of traditional hierarchical labelling systems. Much of it starts with the image of 'the guy in the corner' office, something that is perpetuated throughout much of the corporate world by bricks and mortar.

The layout of the majority of office buildings serves quite literally to reinforce a management structure, from the executive suites on the top floor all the way down to the 'lower level' employees on the ground floor or in a windowless basement.

At Virgin we have studiously avoided having a glass and concrete world headquarters with the bosses lodged in upper-level corner offices. In my own case I have spent my career staying away from offices and have only ever worked from three places: houseboat, home and hammock. Our companies also all work from their own very individual locations and the address of the closest thing we have to a group headquarters says it all: 'The Old Schoolhouse' is anything but a corporate cathedral.

I have long been a big fan of open-plan offices with lots of communal brainstorming spaces, lounges, play areas, pool tables and kitchen areas where co-workers naturally come together and chew the fat. Office walls, doors, desks and counters are nothing but barriers to communication.

But back to the trouble with 'the boss': the old militaristic image of the general bossing his troops from far behind the front line, as opposed to leading them into battle, is not that different from the way many companies are still run today. Make no mistake: a leader is a very different animal from a boss.

If you aren't frequently out there in the front line, leading the charge in lockstep with your employees, you simply cannot stay in touch with the realities of your business. Sitting in the boardroom listening to even the most comprehensive reports from the front can never compare with being there to see it and hear it first-hand.

Latin was never my favourite subject at school – in fact, I don't think I had such a thing – but one word in the Latin class that registered with me was the verb 'educere'. I remember being greatly surprised to learn that the root of the word 'education' actually means 'to lead forth'. Until that moment I had thought of education as 'cramming in' but in reality it is supposed to be about 'leading out'. While a bad school teacher, like a bad boss, will indeed teach or manage by cramming their opinions into their charges, a good educator or corporate leader will do the opposite and draw opinions and ideas out of their students or associates.

So next time someone says to you, 'Okay, you're the boss' as they head for your office door, stop them in their tracks with 'Not really, we're all in this together. So come back here and tell me what you'd be doing with this if you were in my place?' Better still, next time go and visit them in their office or sit down with them in the canteen and seek out their opinions on how things are going. Good examples of leadership can be infectious.

Perhaps the new corporate mantra should be 'bosses should be seen and not heard'.

GREAT CUSTOMER SERVICE

Cultural not optional

I possibly get more questions on the subject of people serving people (aka customer service) than any other subject. This one came from Austria.

> **Q:** At every company where I have worked, sooner or later there are always discussions about the value of customer service: what is the return on investment? Do we spend too much money responding to complaints? How do we measure whether our investments in service affect our business?
>
> And while everyone in the company might agree that customer service is key, it is not seen as a very prestigious area in which to work. How can a company keep its staff motivated to provide great service?
>
> *– Christian Sojka, Austria*

A: *A successful business must never lose its focus on its customers and maintaining its standards. A service culture starts at the top so management must be constantly on guard and ready to respond quickly at the first hint of a problem. Thanks to the Internet, the fallout from a badly handled complaint in London can be a talking point in Australia within seconds. When a service issue rears up, the quality of a company's response can have a huge impact on its reputation and long-term success.*

Everyone on the team needs to be concerned about customer issues, and, in some situations, the effort might even be led by the chief executive. In 2010, extreme weather stranded a plane-load of Virgin America passengers on a snow-bound runway in upstate New York for several hours. The small regional airport's lack of equipment and manpower was compounded by the abnormally high number of planes on the ground and there was simply no safe way to get the passengers off the plane. Immediately on learning about the situation CEO David Cush jumped into the fray and began calling many of the stranded passengers, offering apologies and vouchers for new flights. His personal intervention made a lasting impression on the unhappy customers and also became a big part of the story picked up by the press.

Great communication and customer service, of course, should not be reserved only for emergencies. Keep up a regular dialogue with your customers and front-end staff and it will serve as an early warning system to alert you if a business starts to go off track. I try to read as many letters, good/bad and indifferent, as I can, to get a sense of where our businesses can be improved. I also get a lot of feedback from my followers on Twitter, Google Plus and Facebook.

While some finance directors might not agree, rather than viewing good customer service as strictly a line cost item, it can in many ways be considered a pseudo-marketing expense. It is, after all, the key element in generating good word of mouth, and as everyone knows word of mouth is the best form of advertising – because not only is it highly believable but it is also free!

A good first step to ratcheting up your customer service would be to encourage everyone on your staff to take an active role in coming up with new ideas and solutions to improve the way your company delivers the goods to your customers. Ask your people to experiment and to offer suggestions, and make sure that they are able to do this without worrying about speaking out of turn or being embarrassed in front of their peers – they must be confident that managers will listen to what they have to say. In Virgin we like to say that there is no such thing as a stupid idea! There may be a lot that simply won't work, but that's only after they have been given due consideration. As a manager, I would much rather have the chance to weed through some off-the-wall ideas than fight to maintain the status quo.

Staff at Virgin Active in South Africa, our health club chain, have really taken this approach to heart. The team is challenged to think of ten improvements for every new club we build. One recent staff favourite was the installation in the swimming pools of ladders with six steps rather than the standard four, making it much easier and safer for swimmers to climb in and out of the water. This may seem like an insignificant tweak but the combined effect of many such small changes will make an enormous difference to a customer's experience of your product or service.

In the long run, sustained attention to service can transform how staffers and customers see your business – not just as a place of work or somewhere to visit but as a community. I was told recently a story about David Liebenberg, who works at another of our South African clubs. It seems that as a regular member drove away from the club, David noticed that a brake light was out on his car. The next time that member arrived for a workout the appropriate replacement light bulb was waiting for him. Now that (pun intended) is what I'd call enlightened customer service!

To encourage and build this kind of corporate culture, managers must reward customer service heroes by celebrating their achievements. Soon afterward, David and his wife were given a free weekend stay at a vacation lodge, and the Virgin Active management team then highlighted David's feat as an example in internal education programmes.

Customers shouldn't just think of your business as a place to buy a product or use a service – it should be

a fun place to be! Making customer service key to your organisation
will keep your employees motivated and your customers happy, ensuring enduring loyalty, business success, and, most importantly, a more fulfilling and meaningful experience for all.

CAN BAD NEWS BE GOOD NEWS?

Two-way communication is vital

After an entrepreneur has expanded his successful new company or an executive has been promoted to an even larger corner office, he may sooner or later find himself starting to lose touch with employees and customers.

This happens for a variety of reasons. Most managers will tend to minimise bad news in front of senior executives and emphasise only positive developments in their area of the operation. This in turn forces senior management into perpetually having to read between the lines, and it may leave employees unable to get action on an issue – all because of the fear that admitting to a problem might embarrass a manager or supervisor. Instead, they learn not to ask, but work around the problem while, understandably, griping about management's inability to understand their issues.

So if you find yourself losing touch, one of the best solutions is to take some time to find out what the staff are actually doing on a day-to-day basis. Spend at least a few hours observing operations, and, if you are qualified, grab a widget or another tool and lend a hand. Or if you're visiting the customer service staff, field at least a few customer calls yourself.

As you observe and work, ask yourself: how would I feel if this were my daily work environment? Do people seem energetic and creative? And ask employees: do you have the resources you need to do your job well? If you could, what problems would you fix? What ideas of yours has your manager ever followed up on? Could you do your job from home? Would you like to?

Throughout most organisations, all supervisors, from team leaders to top managers, need periodically to dig in and get their hands dirty. At the executive level, accessibility is key. You must ensure that the staff are consistently encouraged to contact you with ideas and problems. The larger the business, the more important this is.

If you are losing touch with employees, it's also likely that you need to work on maintaining your connection to customers. Most executives and managers tackle this second challenge partly through surveys and other tools that evaluate the customer experience – like letters of complaint. Others, myself included, have embraced social media, keeping clients updated through Facebook, Twitter, YouTube and the rest.

Writing articles or columns is also a new channel for me. To my surprise and delight, I have found that not only has my advice and experience been reaching aspiring entrepreneurs, but also that I, in turn, have been getting a different perspective on our own operations around the world. The hundreds of emails I receive every week bring up a lot of questions, some new ideas and a few telling customer comments – some good, some bad.

One example highlighted how valuable it is to get direct feedback from customers. A Virgin Atlantic flight from Kenya to London was diverted because of heavy snow at Heathrow. It was forced to land in France where, thanks to strict European immigration laws, many of our Kenyan passengers were barred from leaving the airport and had to sleep on camp beds.

The uncomfortable conditions and the unfriendly welcome not unnaturally distressed many of our passengers and I soon received a number of angry emails from Kenyan readers of my column who were either passengers on that flight or who had heard about the ordeal. I wrote an apology that was published in the *Nation* in Kenya, promising we would take up the matter with the French authorities and ensure it could never happen again.

The incident underlined for me the idea that however you can, wherever you can, you must always find ways to keep in touch with your employees and your most far-flung customers. Embrace every opportunity – you never know what you will learn!

Just remember that when you establish or re-establish those relationships with your customers – both internal and external – you are not always going to hear only pleasant news. But as I have mentioned before, the best managers try to catch people doing something right: re-energise your people by showing them that change is possible and action is valued.

If inertia has set in at your company, it's time to show people that their contributions are appreciated. A simple idea can go a long way. When Virgin Active employees expressed a desire to gain experience at other branches, we set up a staff exchange programme. Seven African employees are now working in our European operations; and a related project has resulted in our developing an enhanced pack of information for new employees that has helped to engender greater loyalty right from the start.

CHOOSING A PARTNER

Going down the investor aisle

One of the more common questions I get about starting a company is how one goes about finding investors and picking the right partners.

Entrepreneurs often have a tough time finding someone to fund their venture; many fail to do so but go ahead with the launch anyway, and then they run out of cash. Others find tentative investors who will often renege on promised funding if and when the going gets tough or things don't happen as quickly as they'd hoped. If you can fund it yourself, that's terrific, otherwise locking in a reliable source of start-up capital is fundamental to your business's chances of success.

At the start of my career, I made a conscious effort not to bring in any financial partners, as I wanted to hold all the equity in my businesses. My friends and I worked hard to keep our businesses going using only the cash they generated. For our first business, *Student* magazine, we did all we could to sell advertising up front to pay the bills and, when we started Virgin Records, we handed out leaflets to encourage people to buy records.

This meant that our expansion was slightly slower than we would have liked, but it also meant that I could reward my colleagues with equity in the company. I was free to quickly steer the business in any direction I wanted without having to spend time on distractions like soliciting and waiting for stockholder approval.

The adventures of our early years attracted employees and partners who were drawn in by our spirit and sense of fun. Reflecting on my choices for partners in the music business, I remember they were picked for very practical reasons. One had the biggest record collection I knew of; another could add and subtract better than me; another person always seemed to be able to answer all my constant stream of naïve questions.

Over the years, my partnerships and businesses have grown more sophisticated. Virgin has since joined with many different types of organisations, from large multinationals to professional investors to entrepreneurial management teams looking to wield the Virgin brand as they take on a market. Our experience has shown that, while your prospective partner's ability to fund the venture is important, it is not the essential quality that will sustain the relationship and the business in the long term.

When you are evaluating a proposed investor/partnership, do not focus solely on the capital you need to kick-start your business. Ask: will this person or group give us the space and time we need to build a great business? Bear in mind that a dictatorial financial partner can quickly suck the spirit and enthusiasm out of a new enterprise, muffling the spark that prompted you to launch the project – the spark that is most likely to differentiate your venture from your competitors'.

I have found that our partnerships at Virgin turn out best when we find investors that take a minority stake in a venture and provide capital and support, but leave us to run the business and hire key management.

We have created some great partnerships through Virgin's mobile-phone businesses. In most cases, we found a mobile-telecom operator who wanted to tap into the Virgin brand's strong appeal in order to reach a new segment of the market. The telecom operator would provide the cellular network and, in some cases, some capital; we provided the expertise, branding and people needed to make the new business a reality.

Where the situation has been reversed and Virgin has partnered with a small management team ready to take on a new market sector or territory, I like to think that we have held true to our principles, and given our partners the time, space and capital they needed to build their businesses.

Virgin Active, our health club business, has been built in partnership with the founding management team of Frank Read and Matthew Bucknall. Over the past twelve years, we have completed several acquisitions together, expanding into six countries. Virgin Active is now a leading business in the sector, and Matthew is chief executive. Virgin supplied the brand equity, the reputation and sometimes the capital that the business needed; the management team provided the industry knowledge, the local expertise and, above all, the passion and commitment to make it all work.

Overall, you need to ensure that your people are inspired and have the freedom to be creative. After all, the success of your new business depends upon your most important partnership: the one with your staff.

If you get such partnerships right, your chances of success are much higher. Just as you will need the freedom to build your company according to your vision, they will need the freedom to develop their own areas according to the requirements of your customers and the other employees. Whether or not they will have this independence, which is integral to the business's future success, depends upon your choice of financial partner.

So remember: a partner who just brings in capital is very useful, but a strategic partner who can also provide you and your team with the space, time and freedom needed to build the business is a true friend – and one who is much more likely to stand the test of time.

INVEST IN YOUR PEOPLE

And they'll invest in you

How a new company treats its customers is often the deciding factor in whether it will be successful. Great businesses – the ones who have got it right – are masters at turning customers into advocates for their companies. This means that their marketing efforts are supported by customer word-of-mouth and boosted by positive comments on review sites and social media channels – some of the most important influences on people's buying habits today.

Many of the world's most successful businesses provide terrific customer service. The adulation some of Apple's established customers have for the brand and its products is not only a result of the company's groundbreaking innovations; those products were backed by top-notch customer service. Apple's front-line people are known to be energetic and knowledgeable, which ensures that few customers ever have a bad experience at an Apple store, and most return to buy the latest device.

The retention of customers is important to any company; after all, it makes more sense to keep the good customers you have than to continually chase new ones. In the travel sector, companies have to take customer service seriously if they hope to succeed, because a wonderful flight, train journey – or soon, we hope, space trip – begins and ends with great service. While a company may be able to find ways to improve the interiors of their planes or trains, perhaps installing more comfortable seats and serving better meals, that expensive technology and luxurious design will count for nothing if customer service is shoddy.

Consider how many times you have complained how badly you were treated by a major company when in reality you were talking about a bad experience you had with single employee of that business. I was recently reminded of how important customer service is for all businesses, whether new or long-established, when I visited Virgin America to officially open their training simulator in Burlingame, just outside San Francisco. At Virgin, where our brand is built on the promise of providing terrific service, our flight crews are our most important asset – without them we would be just another airline. The new $1 million simulator is crucial to our expansion plans.

Not every business needs to build a training facility; indeed, many do not need high-tech solutions. But after reconnecting with the team at Virgin America and seeing how they go about training their new people I came away with three key lessons.

I. An investment in your people is an investment in your company

All airlines must ensure that everyone, from pilots to ground workers, has rigorous operational, safety, security and even medical training, but at Virgin America that's just the beginning. Our staff must also complete a broader immersion in brand values through a two-day annual 'brand bath', which the company calls Refresh. At those retreats, they focus on improving customer experience across the airline.

The flight crews are brought together with colleagues from different departments and trained in conflict resolution, hospitality and emotional intelligence training. The programme is designed to help employees truly to understand the customer's perspective; to resolve issues and not push them up the chain.

As an entrepreneur, how can you bring your team together to solve problems and build their trust in each other? At a small business or start-up, this might be accomplished with a low-tech solution, like starting a tradition of having lunch together every Friday and reviewing how the week went.

2. Lead from the front

At Refresh, David Cush, the CEO of Virgin America, often holds question and answer sessions with employees to ensure that he personally addresses their concerns. This is the first step in building bonds between front-line staff and senior managers, which helps to create easy and open communications.

Executives and managers who want to learn how to improve their operations must step away from their desks and get to know their staff. If your company is too big for regular meetings, spending a few hours handling customer complaints yourself or working on the factory floor will help you to understand what's really going on.

3. Make sure employees have the tools they need to succeed

The training at Refresh teaches Virgin America employees to learn how to solve problems on their own – a key to great customer service. This is an unusual approach; most businesses impose restrictions on their staff in terms of the types of problems employees can solve and the authority they have to do so. But our experience shows that the best solution is to provide people with the skills and confidence they need to deal with problems on their own, without sticking to a script or following a flow chart (aka 'passing the buck').

Most often, the missing ingredient is information. If, in your meetings with your staff or during your time on the factory floor, you notice that employees are groping for answers, it is time to take action. Remove limits on access to databases; invest in new information technology; do whatever it takes to make sure that they can seize the initiative on their own.

In tough times, when your competitors are cutting costs, it might be tempting to follow their lead and cut back on customer service. But remember that slashing prices is not the only solution. Every customer is valuable; in the long term, a thriving company is built on relationships, not just the bottom line.

THE DAY THE MUSIC DIDN'T DIE

From vinyl to CD to digital to ...

In business, change sometimes happens more quickly than you want it to – transformative technologies arrive suddenly on the market, tastes adjust, economies shift. Telling your staff to embrace change and get creative is all well and good, but that will not address their (or your) underlying anxieties. The bald fact is that change is usually a threat – one that has the potential to bring your business to a halt.

Let's face it: no company lasts forever. But the advances that technology has brought to the music business are enough to make anyone's head spin faster than a 33⅓rpm LP. And if you are asking 'a what?' you prove my point!

Given Virgin's long experience in the music industry, I often receive questions from readers about the industry's future. What will happen next? How can anyone successfully launch a business in this sector when transformative change is stressing even the nimblest players?

Our experience shows that there is always opportunity in times of change. Those pundits who have spent the past ten years predicting the end of the record industry should remember the last time it was in meltdown: 1982. The economic recession was having a deep impact. Many people were home-taping off the radio or from a friend who had bought the LP – a forerunner to illegal downloading.

At the time, Virgin Retail had over a hundred record stores across the UK. On Saturdays they were jammed, on weekdays they were deserted, on Sundays they were closed. Then along came compact discs.

The new format's advantages were immediately obvious. It was much smaller than the LP, and there was no wear, distortion or surface noise. My notebooks from that period are full of questions about the potential impact on our business. I wrote: 'What happens to the record collection around the country – do people replace their vinyl with CDs?'

At first the only way for us to survive the CD menace was to start clearing the decks for the new stocks, so we started discounting our LPs. We succeeded in switching our business over to CDs, which not all our competitors did.

We could also see that another new retailing phenomenon was dawning. Two years after the introduction of the personal computer in 1980, there were already nearly 500,000 video-game machines in use in the UK. Soon, selling games and then DVDs became a worthwhile sideline for our stores.

By 1986, even Virgin Megastores was under threat. Our biggest rival, HMV, was going after us by opening giant stores, some near our flagship locations. Undeterred, we launched our Dublin store, which at the time was the biggest in the world. That store not only stocked hard-to-find specialist classical and jazz, folk and rock music, but also sold music videos, games and computer software. This was where I could see the future of our business.

And we gave the old-fashioned retailers, such as Woolworths, Dixons and Currys a run for their money. Our shop windows and store interiors were dynamic and exciting. We brought in bands to perform and sign autographs. These events attracted more sales and better publicity.

To make a long story very short, both despite and because of the disruptive change that had just taken place, we transformed our business model and did very well in the eighties and nineties. Music produced by Virgin Records enthralled listeners around the world, many of whom went to Virgin Megastores to buy copies.

Did all this work make us future-proof? Of course not. The truth is that, even from the start, our smaller Virgin Records shops made very little money. The stores kept our name in the public eye, and represented our youthful, irreverent brand, but they were unsustainable in the long run. One of my biggest business mistakes – indeed, regrets – was not selling all of our stores sooner. Closing the book on our record label Virgin Records in 1992, with the sale to EMI, was painful, but the best decision.

But is digital downloading killing music? Well, the economics of actually producing the music today are far healthier than they ever were in Virgin's heyday as a music company. When we built our recording studio, it was a massive, expensive undertaking. Virgin Records' job was to bankroll recording sessions for musicians – and take the risks. To make money, we had to sell a lot of albums.

Now a top-quality album can be made on a laptop, and then you can send the file over the Internet to anyone, almost anywhere. Promotion is as easy as setting up a page on Facebook or another social networking site. Economies of scale don't matter any more to young musicians, although they still matter a great deal to the record companies and their shareholders.

If I were a happening band on the cusp of success, I wouldn't go through a conventional record company today. I'd gather a small team of people and release the tracks or album myself. I would consider getting together with like-minded musicians and sharing distribution, advertising and marketing costs.

Smaller and newer bands earn less, because record companies are only able to promote lesser-known bands by using some of the proceeds from their major artists. With music margins under pressure, there is less money being spent on newer bands and so many will be better off trying it on their own and using the internet to get a following first.

I do think that record companies will survive, but they will have to be much leaner – and, in business, small is beautiful. Those smaller companies will have to discover genuine talent, which is the reason that many people who are passionate about music choose careers in the industry. And with all that energy and zeal to draw on, there's no telling what some entrepreneurs will achieve next.

By the way, that '33^1/$_3$rpm LP' was a 'long-play' 12-inch vinyl record that played at thirty-three and a third revolutions per minute on a turntable. Okay, don't worry about it – the iPod is a lot easier!

GOOD TRAINING
Is good business

Q: When does your staff find time to pursue further training? Do you allow them to do this during normal office hours, or must they do it over the weekend? At our business, we struggle to find time for education during office hours.

– Hans Cahling, Sweden

A: *Ensuring that your team has the tools needed to succeed in an increasingly competitive and challenging marketplace is key for start-ups and emerging companies, as is developing and retaining a strong, stable workforce – this often makes the difference between success and failure.*

But it can be a challenge, since businesses fighting to gain a foothold in their markets can rarely afford for their staff to take time off for training purposes – many do not have enough people to cover for missing workers. Starving your team of training is, however, a false economy. As you build your business, you'll make investments in many different areas so that it can improve and develop; investments in your staff should be at the top of the list.

Finding a good solution will help you to establish your reputation in your industry. It is almost always best to be known as a progressive company, with a strong focus on training, the flexibility to accommodate employees' needs and the guts to stick by them through thick and thin. While doing this might not be easy in today's economic environment, it may be worth any short-term hardship because your company will attract some of the best people in the business, and they will help you to stay ahead of the competition.

At all the Virgin companies we encourage our people to take training days and to develop their skills during business hours. This is not really something that you can expect people to undertake just in the evenings or on weekends. A simple way to tackle the problem of managing on-the-job training is for you to challenge conventions about where and when work is done – legacies of the days when limitations on communications technology required that all employees work in the same place at the same time. I have never believed that the best work is done in a certain building between nine and five and you may find that this is true for your staff as well.

These days, many people can work from home, which permits them to spend more time with their families. Someone who would like to pursue extra training may

*benefit from the flexibility you have established; more
employees may be available to fill in if your office hours
are more flexible. Another option start-ups might consider
is intra-company training, or internal internships, which
can improve skills while keeping staff levels the same.*

*In Virgin's early days, we were similarly challenged
in terms of resources, but I was keen to allow people
to maintain a good work–life balance. I led the way by
working from my home on a houseboat, then from my
house in London. Over time, I invited others to come and
work at my home. That home was damaged by fire in
2001, but I like to think that the family-style environment
helped to sustain the brand's image among its employees
and to reassure them that it was okay to work from home,
if that is what they needed to do.*

*If an employee needs more advanced training that
will require them to leave for longer periods of time, do
everything you can to make sure it happens, perhaps by
looking at options for part-time work. Most simply cannot
afford to take time off, but this is nevertheless an area
in which you should offer your staff further options and
flexibility. Another is offering phased 'retirement' to allow
older staff members to gradually wind down their input
whilst they stay involved, training the next generation to
pick up the baton.*

*Once that element of the employee's training is
complete, you'll need to help that person find ways to hone
their new skills. At Virgin, we encourage transfers to other*

businesses within the group. If this isn't an option, offer your employees temporary assignments that will allow them to show everyone what they can do.

So, when you are worried about further training, don't panic! Take a deep breath, and start working on solutions. Because that ambition is an opportunity: for you to increase your staff's skills, loyalty, motivation and experience, and to establish your company as the best in the business – the best employer, and a market leader: not a bad deal!

Oh, and don't forget. Training is not a one-off thing. To stay on top of market developments, recurrent training and refresher courses should be an ongoing part of company life – and budgets.

REBRANDING
The pros and cons

Q: Many companies spend a lot of money on rebranding. Is changing a business's name necessary when there is a change in ownership? And is it okay to have one brand for all your companies? Can it affect customer confidence in the various products and services one may offer?

– Tanga Roy, Kenya

This question was perfectly timed as I had just spent three amazing days travelling around the UK to mark the launch of Virgin Money, our new bank. Northern Rock is a British bank that was nationalised in 2008 and we acquired it from the government in 2012.

We plan to rebrand Northern Rock's seventy-five branches and in the process this will provide us with a distinctive platform for shaking up the moribund British banking industry. There will be new signs, new furniture and a more welcoming feel – our staff will not be working behind glass barricades.

Those will be the first steps, but the new brand must go deeper, into the very culture of the business, providing leadership, inspiration and a spirit of empowerment to the two thousand people of Northern Rock who have just joined Virgin Money and the Virgin family of companies.

That said, we were concerned about changing the Northern Rock name, mostly because the bank is very well known, especially in the north-east of England – we worried that this might create animosity among longtime customers and long-term employees, who were rightfully proud of their company. But to our delight we found nothing but genuine enthusiasm and excitement at the launch events, and the Virgin team was made very welcome.

While the decision about if and when to rebrand a company we acquire depends on many factors, we have found that, far from hindering our growth, branding Virgin businesses with our name has helped them to punch well above their weight while creating a very distinctive culture that ties our group of companies together, across its variety of sectors. Virgin Money is now set to leverage Virgin's brand equity as the cornerstone for a marketing campaign for the rebranded Northern Rock – the ads will show how we have challenged many diverse industries to make things better.

Our approach to branding has been successful because we have built the Virgin Group on a simple mission: to do things differently for our customers, improving their experiences and perhaps their lives. It should not matter whether you are on one of our planes or trains, a member of one of our health clubs or talking to a friend using one of our mobile phone services: the experience should stand out as distinctly Virgin.

Customers asked to describe the Virgin experience might point to our staff's cheery helpfulness; our focus on thoughtful, simple design; the way we add a human touch wherever possible; and our humour as well. The whole package should make customers feel good about our brand and want to return for more.

Maintaining customer confidence is key to any brand, and so, whenever we consider rebranding an existing company, we take a close look at the business proposition, the service and the quality and training of the people before planting our distinctive logo and splash of red.

When we were preparing to launch Virgin Trains in the late nineties, industry executives laughed at our plans to build a new fleet of tilting trains, and to provide better food and service – along with our goal of doubling passenger numbers. This was impossible, we were told. And since we couldn't get our hands on new trains for several years (they are not a stock item!), we had no option but to repaint the 'well used' railway carriages we'd inherited from British Rail.

One of our first steps was training our new team to change the way they dealt with customers, and this proved to be the best rebranding effort possible; our terrific staff helped our customers through the difficult period of delays and repair work. In the years that followed, our new fleet of trains, modernised track and faster journeys helped our employees to deliver better than ever, and we achieved among the highest customer service ratings in the industry. Customer numbers have more than doubled since 2006 – from 14 million to over 30 million.

When we were preparing to launch Virgin Media in 2006, which was intended to offer cable, Internet, mobile phone and landline services, we took a more cautious approach. Rather than rebranding the company right away, we ensured that the two companies that merged to create NTL:Telewest got their new product and customer service levels about right and had completed their merger with Virgin Mobile – before we embarked on the major rebrand to Virgin Media. We did this in part because we were worried that NTL:Telewest could not yet achieve the level of service expected of a Virgin business. The company provided broadband, cable and phone service to more than five million homes: any disruption or poor service delivered under the Virgin name would have affected our other businesses.

After more than a year, we rebranded NTL:Telewest as Virgin Media and, four years later, the company had trained the staff, refocused its business proposition and improved its products. It is now investing heavily in its 'Virgin-ness', including an advertising campaign with Usain Bolt, the world's fastest sprinter, pretending to be me.

Finally, if you are considering whether to put your brand on a business your company has recently acquired, remember to share your message with your new employees about your purpose and culture. Meet with them, take notes on their suggestions and follow through. With their support and enthusiasm, you will win over customers, build your company's expertise, expand what your business has to offer and derive maximum value from this rebranding.

SOCIAL SERVICES REDEFINED
Viral virgins all

The brave new world of Twitter and Facebook is something that I have had to learn about very quickly in the last few years and this question from Colombia is typical of many I get asked these days.

> **Q: We've been trying to find a way to improve communication with our customers, but neither our website nor our Facebook page is producing results. What would you suggest?**
>
> *– Billy Loaiza Rivera, Colombia*

> **A:** *This is a question keeping many chief executives and company founders awake at night as they struggle to keep up with rapid changes in the digital world.*
>
> *The swift rise of communication channels such as Facebook and Twitter has caused many executives to reassess how they stay in touch with their customers, with*

employees and, increasingly, with the media itself.

Companies' relationships with their customers have dramatically and suddenly changed. People no longer want to be sold to; they want companies to help them find an informed way to buy the right product or service at the right price. They still watch ads, but often online rather than on TV, and they're much more likely to view ads that friends have recommended. When something goes wrong with a product, they want to be able to reach the company instantly, and they expect – no – demand, quick solutions.

How companies adapt to this energetic and sometimes chaotic world will define their future success. The website Google plus, Facebook page, blog and Twitter feed are no longer add-ons to a business's communication budget: they have to be central to its marketing strategy, and used in coordination with other marketing efforts.

As a first step in addressing your problem, make sure that your site is set up not just to handle transactions, but also for communication – and that when customers leave comments or send emails your team always follows up. Look at every contact as an opportunity to build stronger relationships with your customers. Depending on the channels you choose, this might mean helping your customer service staff adapt to new methods of communicating. Once they have, you must continue to keep in touch with customers yourself.

In the past, I would ask Virgin customers to write to me with problems or ideas, and I often called people to talk about the problems that came up. It was and is a great way to check on our businesses' quality and standards – though many of the complainants believed one of their friends was playing a practical joke on them. To this day, I try to answer as many emails as I can and encourage our executives to do the same.

Neil Berkett, the chief executive of Virgin Media, our UK cable and telecom group, recently told me that he gets twenty to thirty emails a day from customers, and he tries to respond with a brief, direct note within hours. This has helped him improve the company's reputation for customer service, which certainly needed a lot of work when we first combined NTL:Telewest and Virgin Mobile to create Virgin Media in 2007.

Beyond customer service, you may need to consider that the old divisions between advertising, marketing and public relations have completely rearranged themselves so it's time to review how your marketing team works. Virgin Atlantic recently created a social relations team to manage the combined media space and to make sure our sites and communications are current and interesting, maintaining the cheeky, irreverent flair that characterises the brand.

We have always tried to maximise the impact of our advertising through clever PR, daring stunts and amusing media campaigns. The rise of social media has presented some exciting challenges to the status quo and caused us to question our usual ways of doing business.

When we launched a new global ad for Virgin Atlantic on TV and in cinemas – full of humour, fun and with a touch of glamour – it also started to generate a big following online, as it was promoted by our fans to their friends. This extended the reach of our ad far beyond our usual audiences. It also ensures that the people see and hear our advert. Amusingly, I was in the cinema recently and could not hear the sound on the adverts. I asked an attendant what was wrong, and was told they often turn the sound down to allow people to chat before the film. Only problem was – I gently pointed out – they had blanked out two Virgin ads! The next time I went in they were deafeningly loud!

To succeed, such efforts must be supported from the top. I have taken digital very seriously and with more than 5 million followers, I have found it invaluable when campaigning on social issues such as drug reform or the banning of shark finning – as well as promoting the latest news from our companies. David Cush at Virgin America freed up the management of these channels from the company's classic hierarchy. His social media team is made up of twenty-somethings who have been selected to run the online services. David says they were given broad guidelines and then let loose.

These employees, who were 'born digital', have placed Facebook and Twitter at the centre of the company's communication strategy, capturing the Virgin spirit online. Recently the American Society for the Prevention of Cruelty to Animals contacted Virgin America to ask if we would help fly chihuahuas from California to the East Coast. It seems West Coast shelters were so full of this breed of dog that they had a better chance of finding homes elsewhere. We agreed straightaway. Some of our caring crew members even volunteered to accompany the homeless pups, and we sent them off in style on a flight from San Francisco to New York.

The team promoted this story through all channels. It instantly went viral and also sparked the interest of the traditional media – drawing attention to the ASPCA and Virgin America's efforts to help. We then used the story as the basis of a very successful online sale of flights to Mexico – chihuahua, think about it!

To succeed, entrepreneurs and business leaders must look at this digital world through a different lens; by working with your online sites, services and teams, you can transform these challenges into opportunities.

He who resists can only lose!

A-B-C-D
Always Be Connecting Dots

I am often asked about what appears to be a fairly high level of vertical integration within the Virgin Group's scores of businesses – a situation in which many ventures are united under a common owner. My customary, half-joking response is usually that we prefer to see it as 'vertical disintegration'.

Don't get me wrong: I don't mean to imply that our group is falling apart – quite the opposite! We continue to grow and enter new business sectors at a healthy clip. While a lot of these new ventures may appear to observers to be utterly tangential – as when we were an independent record label and we started an international airline; later we got into mobile phone services and health clubs – over time the synergies usually become apparent. So if 'disintegration' sends the wrong message, a better way to describe our philosophy of growth is the ABCD process: as in 'Always Be Connecting Dots'.

It's rather like those drawing books where children connect sequentially numbered dots, eventually creating a picture that wasn't at all obvious at first glance. Connecting the first few dots is usually more difficult, and then, as in business, when the big picture starts to emerge, finishing the puzzle usually gets a lot easier.

When we launched Virgin Atlantic in 1984 there wasn't any obvious connection between our company, which was then Virgin Records, and the airline industry. At the time the level of service being offered by the world's airlines was just so awful that we felt there was a huge opportunity for a company ready to put some effort into doing things better. It just so happened that, as we were already in the entertainment business, we naturally brought what we knew best – how to entertain our customers – to an industry that was desperately in need of precisely that tweak.

We equipped our planes to provide great audio and video entertainment; assembled a fun, happy cabin crew who actually enjoyed looking after their customers; designed comfortable, contemporary interiors; and then sold the experience at a highly competitive fare. Suddenly the dots connected and Virgin Atlantic was the cool new way to travel and the talk of the airline industry.

When we first ventured into mobile phone services, we really didn't know much about the business, but saw an opportunity to disrupt the market, particularly by focusing on the needs of young people. At the time most of the big carriers were focused on selling monthly contracts to adults. Parents of teenagers and college students were usually loath to let their kids have mobiles because they so often exceeded their talk and text limits, racking up big charges on their parents' accounts.

Through Virgin Mobile, we returned the focus to the customer, instead of only competing on minutes and rates. We offered parents the option of setting a credit limit on a phone and keeping it topped up to that level, which meant that none of our customers had the experience of opening a phone bill at the end of the month and discovering unanticipated charges in the hundreds of pounds. As with the airline, we had seen an opportunity to take advantage of our strengths in customer service and simply connected the dots – as well as a lot of phone calls and texts.

Diversification is often a terrifying concept for executives at other companies and they usually have a story or three to tell about 'here's why we stick to our knitting'. If you listen to those stories, there's usually a common denominator: even if you are the best knitters in the industry, when you enter a new sector that has no relationship to balls of yarn, you shouldn't march in brandishing your knitting needles and declare, 'This is the way we do things around here'.

When we boldly venture into new businesses about which we know next to nothing, we always hire people who know the sector well, but who, like us, also understand that it is ready to be shaken up. The right people will be capable of connecting even the same old basic dots in such innovative ways that a wholly different, quite distinctive, picture will emerge.

So there's no great secret to our launching or partnering with what seem to be unconnected businesses. That's not to say it's easy, but by sticking to our core brand values of delivering superb customer service, bringing together terrific people and engaging in unbridled innovation, we have found that there are very few businesses with which a connection cannot be made and learned from. And these experiences strengthen the group as a whole, allowing us to make new connections.

Looking back, I am always flabbergasted at just how well all the Virgin dots line up with each other. We now have brand loyalists who fly with us, work out with us, use our mobile phone and broadband services, take our trains, drink our wines, watch our films and now can even bank with us.

We also once had a knitting company at Virgin. It was called Black Sheep and was run by my Aunt Clare but, as you may have surmised, we simply didn't stick with it.

Remember **A-B-C-D**! You will end up in the most amazing places.

EMPOWERMENT AND APPRECIATION

Both go a long way

I recently received a very interesting letter:

> **Q. How far should you go to please a client? At some point, there's a risk of compromising your business. How do you keep customers happy without getting hurt in the process? Surely you need rules and regulations?'**
> – *Lee Boss, Kenya*

Great questions. An organisation must establish a clear framework to which employees can refer when carrying out their duties. Such a framework will have to involve written procedures and rules – particularly when cash and accounting are at issue. That said, however, sometimes rules really are made to be broken: the rulebook should not become an excuse for poor customer service or an obstacle to great service. Almost everyone has at some point experienced a situation where a customer service representative has blamed the rules for his inability to help. It will usually begin with 'I'm sorry but the regulations state quite clearly ...'

If your company is going to stand out from the rest because of its truly excellent customer service, staffers should treat the rules more as flexible guidelines, to be followed as the situation demands. The customer is not always right – and neither is the rulebook. The customer service representative's goal should be to strike a balance that serves both the customer's and company's interests in the best way possible.

To a great extent, this can be achieved by empowering customer contact staff to use their common sense when handling questions and problems. Encouraging a good attitude towards problem solving is crucial, but so is a corporate culture that rewards initiative and does not discourage a creative approach.

One customer service mantra that I have always loved is 'First to know, first to handle'. In other words, when a problem arises, there is a fleeting opportunity to solve it on the spot. One great example of this comes from Virgin America, when a flight was delayed in San Francisco. While the passengers waited for news, the crew brought the drinks trolley out to the gate and served drinks to the guests. A few months later, I called into an all-employee meeting to award that crew with a 'Vammy' Virgin America's annual staff award.

Resolving problems this way has multiple benefits for both the customer and the company. For the customer, the advantages are obvious: the problem is solved, or at least alleviated. And for the company there is an obvious public-relations benefit: the customer is likely to tell other people how well the situation was handled. There are also significant cost benefits – for example, a reduction in the number of back-office customer relations staffers required to handle the usually protracted back and forth process for resolving formal customer complaints.

At Virgin, a few senior managers and I host an annual 'Stars Dinner' to recognise top performers – staff members who have been nominated by their peers – and celebrate their achievements. I haven't missed one yet. We look for the best examples of customer service, innovation, community service and environmental work. This kind of event demonstrates to employees that you care about them and that you notice and appreciate their hard work and initiative.

In the world of customer service, nice words from a supervisor are relatively easy to come by; the real proof is in positive feedback from customers. That's when you know that the right kind of culture is taking hold.

I was particularly pleased by a note I received recently from Phil Williamson, a Virgin customer in Kenya who wrote to me about a trip to London he'd booked with his wife. Shortly before the trip, Phil's wife was travelling for business and was able to meet Phil in London using a plane ticket she'd received from a client. So they put her original ticket aside to use another time, but later, when they tried to book a new flight using that ticket, they found that it had expired because they hadn't paid a change fee.

Hawa, a Virgin representative in Kenya, explained the Williamsons' situation to an accountant, who evidently told her that rules are rules, and that the airline could not make an exception in this case. In the end, though, Hawa appealed to another supervisor, the ticket was refunded and a new one was purchased.

'All's well that ends well,' Phil told me. 'But wouldn't it have been so much better if the accountant had displayed a little more general business sense instead of sticking to his strict interpretation [of the rules]?'

This tale aptly demonstrates how close organisations come to losing customers every day, due to rigid adherence to rules and not enough thought on the part of a few front-line employees. Keep in mind this classic statistic: an unhappy customer will tell ten people about a problem, while a satisfied customer will only tell four people about a good experience.

So, work on developing a corporate culture that tries to 'catch employees doing something right' and rewards dedication and initiative. Empowering and taking care of your staff is the best way to look after your customers and keep them coming back for more.

LAUNCHING
A BUSINESS
Four common mistakes

When talking with young entrepreneurs, one of the questions I get asked most often is about the pitfalls they will face. What are the most common mistakes that entrepreneurs make when starting out?

Asking about mistakes is a good sign because, while making them is a big part of the process of building a company, quickly recovering from them is what's most important. It's all part of the adventure of entrepreneurship, which will require all of your stamina, drive and determination.

But your way forward is not entirely uncharted: when you notice an opportunity that has never occurred to anyone else, there are certain steps to turning your vision into reality. You must formulate an innovative business plan, find funding, hire the right people to carry out the plan and then step back from your role in the business at exactly the right moment.

Let's take a look at these steps, and also at ways to avoid some of the most common mistakes new entrepreneurs make.

Step One: Stay on Target

A mistake often associated with the first step is signalled by an entrepreneur's inability to clearly and concisely communicate their idea. You have to be able to generate buy-in from investors, partners and potential employees, so nail down your 'elevator speech' – what you would say if you ran into an important potential investor and had literally only two minutes to tell your story. Try using a Twitter-like template to refine the essence of your concept into just 140 characters. Once you've done that, expand your message to a maximum of 500 characters. Remember, the shorter your pitch, the clearer it will be.

An associated error is lack of focus. If your start-up has been tagged as 'the next big thing', the adrenaline rush that comes with building buzz can lead to impetuous decisions and a loss of a sense of purpose. Many entrepreneurs end up sprinting in many directions instead of taking assertive steps towards their target. Clearly define your goals and strategies and then establish a timeline. Don't let the other possibilities or hazy dreams distract you from achieving your goal.

Getting too far ahead of yourself is also dangerous. If your product or service is still on the drawing board, don't get sidetracked by plans for future versions. As a general guideline, looking two or three years ahead is best, but the nature of your business and feedback from your investors will help you determine just how far ahead you should plan.

Be flexible, because, just as lack of planning can be a problem, adhering blindly to your plan is a sure-fire way to steer your company off a cliff. A successful entrepreneur will constantly adjust course without losing sight of the final destination.

Step Two: Be realistic about costs

Don't short-change your start-up when estimating the funds you will require – you'll just diminish your chances of success. Keeping your expenses under control is vital, but don't confuse capitalisation with costs. The playing field is littered with undercapitalised start-ups that were doomed from the outset.

Start-ups almost always draw up plans that are seriously underbudgeted on overheads. When you have come up with a number for your overheads, don't just tack on 10 per cent for contingencies, add 75 per cent or double it! You are guaranteed to have overlooked any number of hidden costs, fees and taxes.

David Neeleman knew this. In 1998 he told me he needed $160 million in start-up capital for what would eventually emerge as JetBlue – a huge sum, much more than any other start-up airline had ever raised. Most of the so-called experts scoffed at the notion that he would be able to find the money and launch a low-cost airline when established companies were failing one after the other. However, he stuck to his guns and raised the money. As a result, JetBlue had one of the most successful airline launches of all time, and turned a profit only six months after its launch in 2000. (It was very nearly called Virgin Blue, but that's another story.)

Step Three: Hire the people you need, not the people you like

As tempting as it may be to staff your new business with friends and relatives, this is likely to be a serious mistake. If they don't work out, asking them to leave will be very tough.

When Virgin starts any new business, we always hire a core team of smart people who already know the industry and its inherent risks. Take full advantage of the knowledge pool you've created; when a problem comes up, remember that nobody has all the answers, including you.

One of your goals should be to find a manager who truly shares your vision, and to whom you can someday confidently hand the reins so that you can carry out the next step.

Step Four: Know when to step down as CEO

A great entrepreneur knows when the time has come to leave the CEO role. It's seldom easy, but it has to be done: very few entrepreneurs make great managers. In my own case, managing the daily operations of a business simply isn't in my DNA (or, as I've said to friends, 'It's not bloody likely').

Stepping back doesn't mean turning your back on your business. At Virgin, I'm always involved in the launch of a new business, and then I gradually hand over control to the new management team as it starts to jell. But no matter how long it has been since I was at the helm, if I see something that I don't like I'm not at all shy about making my thoughts known and asking some very pointed questions.

Founders shouldn't hesitate to reinsert themselves into their businesses when necessary – look at Larry Page, who returned as CEO at Google. That said, I had to laugh when I heard this news, wondering how many managers at Virgin businesses had thought, 'Wow, I hope this Google thing doesn't give Richard any ideas.'

It didn't!

KEEP AN EYE ON THE DETAILS

The Devil rests there too

So you have an idea for a business – one that you believe has the potential to alter the industry. You have put together a simple, straightforward proposition that potential customers find easy to understand. You have raised the necessary capital, gathered a team and publicised your new venture by every means available. What happens next?

It's time to deliver on your promises. And the only difference between merely satisfactory delivery and great delivery is an obsessive attention to detail. Every detail – no matter how seemingly insignificant!

Anyone who aspires to lead a company must develop a habit of taking notes. As I've said, I carry a notebook everywhere I go but an iPad would work just well. Most of my entries are like this one, from a Virgin Atlantic flight years ago: 'Dirty carpets. Fluff. Equipment: stainless steel, grotty. Choice of menu disappointing – back from Miami, prawns then lobster (as a main course) in Upper Class. Chicken curry very bland. Chicken should be cut in chunks. Rice dry. No Stilton on cheeseboard.'

What's most revealing is this final note: 'Staff desperate for someone to listen. Make sure flight staff reports are actioned IMMEDIATELY.' I'm pleased to say that they have been ever since. This is the real key to getting all the other items on the list done – employees who are enabled to report problems and get them fixed – before I come along with my notebook.

And as you decide how best to deliver your product or service, keep in mind the company's core business values, the short- to medium-term strategic considerations and where the industry is heading in the long term. Make your decisions on the micro level in light of that bigger picture and your business should be heading in the right direction.

Owners and leaders of established companies should sample their business's products as often as possible. Many bosses regularly speak to staff at all levels, but often fail to follow up on problems they uncover. This means that their employees never learn what importance the CEO places on getting the details right, or see just how necessary and possible it is to address the everyday problems that come up. If you foster a corporate culture of waiting for someone else to solve problems, the company will suffer the consequences.

Great delivery also depends on great communication, which should start at the top. Be brave: hand out your email address and phone number. Your employees will know not to misuse it or badger you, and, by doing so, you will be giving them a terrific psychological boost – they will know that they can contact you anytime a problem comes up that requires your attention.

Instilling attention to detail throughout your new company will prove especially important when the business begins to gain ground. It always tickles me when a spokesman explains to reporters that a company experiencing delays or other problems is 'a victim of its own success' – as though it had undergone something rare and freakish.

The other line that is guaranteed to get my goat is when the excuse for slow service is 'Sorry but we're really busy today'. My reaction is always to say, 'Oh, too bad, but don't worry, keep this up and it won't be a problem much longer'.

Finally, when you do start to see success in the form of a stream of new and repeat business, remember to keep a cool head. You're delivering change, and if you are succeeding, other businesses are very probably getting hurt in the rough and tumble. They will try to shut you down and they will try and emulate what you're doing. So keep moving and improving: laurels are nice but to rest on them is to risk losing your edge.

Be sportsmanlike, play to win and try to avoid nasty confrontations with your enemies. If you do fall out with a partner, colleague or competitor, let the thing cool off then call them and suggest you get together for dinner. It is likely you have a great deal in common. After all, why did you both get into the business in the first place?

THE LONELY
ENTREPRENEUR?

Think again

People tend to think of entrepreneurs as go-it-alone heroes, but this isn't how it works in real life.

Many live up to their reputation as risk-takers and some remain outsiders, but despite this outlier status, entrepreneurs need support to be successful. In fact, we're a lot like Formula 1 drivers: the person in the cockpit gets all the glory while fans tend to forget about the pit crews and all the behind-the-scenes effort it takes to keep the engines running and car and driver on the track. The engine that keeps whole national economies on track is driven by entrepreneurs and small business owners. Together they create jobs, fuel growth and, ultimately, transform communities. This means it's vital that governments, investors and educators find ways to harness this energy source. It also means that encouraging entrepreneurs to start again when a business fails is fundamental to a healthy economy.

For example, an entrepreneur picking himself up after a setback may need a mentor to remind him that this 'what's next?' outlook is everything. My parents taught me from a very young age the importance of maintaining a positive attitude and of taking responsibility for my actions. These are two invaluable building blocks that have shaped my career.

My mother was my first mentor. As a child, I was always impatient to try new challenges whether at home, on the sports field or even at school. When things did not go right (and often they did not!), she would always tell me not to look back in regret, but to move on and try the next thing. I believe this basic attitude is crucial to success in business. Creating a business can be a very tough and lonely experience – many start-ups fail in their early years – but an entrepreneur cannot look at a setback as a bad experience; it's just part of the learning curve.

To help change the world, we need to nurture young people interested in business to develop this entrepreneurial spirit – not an easy task. Universities and colleges can teach some skills, but I think that most budding entrepreneurs would be better off relying on an informal network of coaches and mentors who have the experience (aka 'scars') and expertise needed to coax them forward. I myself rely on an amazing team of advisers, managers and fellow entrepreneurs to help me run the Virgin Group – and, yes, to this day my mother still isn't shy about expressing her opinion on what I get up to! Creating this kind of mentoring environment was very much what we had in mind when we decided to establish the Branson Centre of Entrepreneurship in Johannesburg and Jamaica. It is not so much a school as an incubator of business talent. It is a place where enthusiastic young people with great ideas can absorb practical business skills while at the same time meeting and learning from successful entrepreneurs from around the world.

The class of 2011 had an emphasis on creating jobs in disadvantaged communities in South Africa and Jamaica, and consisted mostly of entrepreneurs hoping to take their existing businesses to the next level.

One great example of a business nurtured by the South African Centre is Gaming Zone. Based in Soweto, near Johannesburg, and founded by Musa Maphongwane and Amos Mtsolongo, Gaming Zone repurposed shipping containers to create safe and affordable places for its customers – local kids – to play the latest video games. Musa and Amos proudly plan to expand to 'hundreds of stores' and also to provide free weekly classes in computer skills that are open to all.

This is a wonderful example of a business that can expand commercially while at the same time making a big impact on the surrounding community – and a perfect example for the new generation of South African entrepreneurs to emulate.

I believe that if we are going to conquer global challenges such as hunger, poverty and climate change, there must be more cooperation, collaboration and shared learning among entrepreneurs. This is why I spend a lot of my time meeting entrepreneurs around the world, looking for great business ideas to foster. This is not just about funding a lot of start-ups;

we work hard to help aspiring entrepreneurs to source funding themselves.

In business, there is no substitute for experience. So if you're an entrepreneur, get on with it. If you've achieved success in business, think about giving back to the community by mentoring some promising entrepreneurs. Who knows? They just might be the next Musa and Amos.

THE PLANET'S PROBLEMS
A world of opportunities

Given the current state of the world economy, entrepreneurs and business leaders may feel that prospects are gloomy for their start-ups and established companies. With the economies of a number of European countries reeling from the debt crisis, the United States Congress struggling to reach an agreement on raising the government's debt ceiling and, with the possibility of another global slowdown on the horizon, some executives are making conservative choices in preparation for still more difficult times ahead.

But this is not the time to play it safe: never let mainstream views about markets affect your thinking on new ventures. Uncertain times are often best for setting up new enterprises – talented employees are primed to try new ideas and suppliers are willing to cut prices in order to bring in new clients and extra sales. The secret is to find a product or service that will stand out by improving people's lives.

A number of people have asked me which industries and sectors entrepreneurs should be looking at in this economic climate. In the past, Virgin has often looked for openings in industries where market leaders were underperforming and not treating their customers properly – as I have pointed out, we have had success in aviation, mobile phone services and financial services. But now we are focusing on the green sector: finding ways to supply renewable energy, produce clean water and figuring out how to conserve both. We believe this area offers the greatest opportunities of our time.

Consider that our society is now facing difficult practical challenges that require innovative, even revolutionary thinking – the staple diet of entrepreneurs. How do we supply enough energy, food and water to meet the demands of our growing global population? How do we lift billions out of poverty without running out of resources? Can we simultaneously restore and protect the natural life-support systems on which we depend?

If you are thinking about entering this sector, try to evaluate where the structural opportunities may lie in your region. There should be openings in nearly every market: the International Energy Agency estimates that global energy consumption will increase by almost 40 per cent over the next twenty years; to meet global demand through 2035, our society will need to make $33 trillion in investments in energy-supply infrastructure.

Major oil producers argue that there is enough oil to meet these needs for many years, but even if that is so – and it's very questionable – climate-change considerations and concerns about the political stability of oil-producing nations mean that government officials around the world need to turn to other options. Before the 2011 tsunami that damaged nuclear power stations in Japan, nuclear power was thought by many to be the strongest alternative, and public agencies and private companies were investing in this area; but now new safety concerns mean there is more emphasis on other sources of renewable energy.

Indeed, analysts predict that renewable sources such as solar, wind, biofuels and hydroelectricity will soon supply a quarter of our energy needs. The latest forecast from the research firm Clean Edge Inc. suggests that combined sales for solar, wind and biofuels will grow from $188.1 billion in 2010 to $349.2 billion by 2020.

If you are located in a region where supplies of fresh water are short, you may want to consider entering that arena. Water shortages are only going to get worse: according to United Nations projections, by 2030 more than 60 per cent of the world's population – five billion people in total – will be living in urban areas. Through Virgin's Green Fund we have invested in a desalination business called Seven Seas Water to create fresh-water supplies in places where there is great need, like the Caribbean. Providing this resource in a sustainable, environmentally sound way is a technical challenge: is your team ready to tackle such an exciting assignment?

Another area that offers opportunities is energy and water efficiency, which includes everything from light bulbs to insulating materials to kitchen taps. This is the most cost-effective means of reducing CO_2 emissions and at the same time making our resources last longer. A recent McKinsey study found that if $170 billion per year is invested in energy efficiency for the next nine years, growth in energy demand will be cut in half – a big step towards reducing CO_2 emissions and avoiding disastrous levels of global warming. If you and your team are looking for rewarding, meaningful work, think about playing your part in securing the future of our planet!

If you are struggling to find funding for your idea for a product or service, or to determine the way forward for your established business, now may be the right time to try something different. Depending on your location and area of expertise, you may decide that your best prospects lie in the green industry. Nations around the world are confronting daunting problems in terms of shortages of water and energy: let's offer some solutions.

'LET'S SHAKE ON THAT'

Now get the lawyers in here

Q: There was a time when shaking hands was enough to close a deal. Do handshakes still have meaning in modern business?

– Winfred Kagwe, Kenya

A: *Well, Winfred, I suppose the answer is 'yes, but …' A handshake is still important to business because trust is central to all relationships. In an ideal world, a handshake would be all that an entrepreneur or executive needs to seal a deal with a business partner, an investor, a company or a client – after all, reputation is everything in life as it is in business. Your word should still be your bond and, if you break your word, your reputation can be irreparably damaged.*

However, the handshake is only the beginning of the process of building a working relationship. Business

*conditions can change dramatically in a very short time
– everything from the state of the economy to consumer
tastes to competitive responses – and interpretations of
how a deal will be applied in different circumstances can
vary wildly.*

*Also, people's recollections change over time.
Conveniently, when the parties to the agreement try to
recall the exact details of a verbal deal years later, it's
like 'Telephone', the children's game where a whispered
phrase is passed from person to person and always turns
out to be wildly different from the original at the end
of the line. This is partly because people are naturally
prone to being too optimistic at a deal's outset, and then,
when dreams meet reality, memory becomes selective
– especially when large sums of money are involved. It
is much more likely you and your partner will fall out if
you have only a handshake agreement, so follow up that
handshake with a clear, simple contract that spells out
the terms of the deal.*

*I learned this early on: in Virgin Records' early days, there
were a number of occasions on which we signed up bands
on the basis of a handshake, only to find out later that our
handshake had been superseded by a written legal agreement
with a competitor. We lost out on deals with bands like Dire
Straits and 10cc for this reason. (The underlying problem
was that in music there are many parties involved in any
deal – band members, agents and advisers can all have very
different agendas.)*

In some cases, we should have updated our agreements to reflect the successes of some deals. When Mike Oldfield came to us with Tubular Bells, we took a significant risk in funding the album's production and distribution. It became an amazing, enduring success, helping to launch our new company. We updated his deal over the years, but, with hindsight, we could have been a bit quicker to revise the terms, for more equitable returns for both parties.

But I had learned that relying on a handshake could be very risky in contentious situations, so our simple legal agreements did allow me to settle issues quickly and, in some cases, to be a little more generous than a contract stipulated. When Nik Powell, my friend and co-founder, decided to step aside from Virgin, we had a basic agreement in place that helped us to decide how to proceed quickly and amicably. I'm glad we had the foresight to put that document together, because we parted friends and have remained so for forty years.

Many entrepreneurs launching their first ventures do not obtain detailed contracts simply because the process is often known to be slow, arduous and expensive and many businesses are launched in a hurry.

Lawyers need to ensure that they cover every eventuality, which may mean they add pages of legal clauses. To try to avoid this situation, when you've reached a deal you and your counterpart should together make a basic outline of your agreement and then pass that document to the lawyers. You'll find that if you take control of these first steps, it is often easier to keep a handle on the drafts – and the legal bills – that follow.

A reputation for being fair and consistent is not just important for entrepreneurs building their businesses; everyone in your company, from the executives to the front-line employees, needs to follow through, continuing to build the relationships created by your agreements. Going the extra mile can make all the difference in establishing your company's reputation. If they're going to do so, however, your people need to know the agreement's terms, so many of them will need to see the contract as well. This is greatly facilitated if you have a short-form 'highlights' version that can be easily read and understood in minutes rather than hours.

So back to the 'yes' part of my answer: please make a point of shaking hands on a deal – but then make sure to ask your lawyers to record the details. It could be the best money you ever spend!

OFFICE RELATIONSHIPS

A touchy subject

In early 2012 I spent several wonderful days meeting the people of Northern Rock in their offices around the UK. As I have said Virgin acquired the bank from the UK government and it – Northern Rock, not the government – is in the process of being rebranded as Virgin Money.

As the 'new owners' one can never be too sure of the reception you might get from the staff at a newly acquired company, but to a person they were all quite delightful. I was there to welcome the Northern Rockers as the newest members of the Virgin family and so was thrilled to discover that a strong family spirit was already very much a part of the fabric of the bank.

Not only was I constantly meeting husbands and wives working in the same office but in several cases sons and daughters, too. I cannot think of a more glowing endorsement of an employer than saying that you have recommended it as a place where your immediate family should also work.

A couple of days after this experience I was having dinner with an old friend from New York who, out of the blue, asked me what Virgin's policy is on what he described as 'office romances'. It seems that his 28-year-old son works at a company that flat-out prohibits office romances and so the young man is having a miserable time trying to keep his three-month relationship with a female co-worker under wraps. Even outside the office they live in fear of being spotted together by an office 'whistle-blower' and it is putting a lot of stress on both of them.

I hadn't thought about the issue before and to the best of my knowledge we have never had any problems with office relationships. We certainly do not have any ridiculous taboos that force people to make a secret of their emotions. Frankly, with people spending more time than ever before in the workplace and first marriages happening much later in life than they once did, falling in love at the office would seem more like an inevitability than a corporate misdemeanour.

My interest was piqued and so I bounced the question off a few heads of what I'd consider progressive companies and have come up with what seems like a sensible approach whereby employers and employees can avoid problems – without shooting Cupid down.

KISS ('Keep it simple stupid') would seem to be applicable in more ways than one here. If single employees are told that they are free to have relationships with any consenting single colleague – single and consenting being the operative words –

then it should be a win-win for company and employee.

By not driving people into covert relationships it should make it a lot easier to gain the respect and compliance of your people with a few practical and simple rules.

For obvious reasons, couples involved in a relationship should ideally not have direct reporting lines one to the other. Also, while every company and situation is different, having both work in the same department may not be a good idea. Too close a day-to-day working relationship, irrespective of how discreet and sensible the couple might be, does tend to invite problems. So some departmental distancing might be good for both.

One interesting suggestion I got was that, 'They should act like a married couple around the office and have no outward displays of affection'. This may be a bit of a lame joke, but it is also wise advice.

One sensible suggestion I heard is not to use company email for passing of what we used to call 'nookie-notes' when I was a kid. Apart from anything else one simple errant stroke of a key can broadcast things to the whole company that are much better kept private!

Come what may, an office relationship can often end up with one participant or the other having to look for a job elsewhere. Ironically, whether the trigger is an unpleasant break-up or a wedding, the outcome can be exactly the same.

So any forward thinking company should think twice about the outright prohibition of office romances. Rather than implementing rules that (as in my friend's son's case) make for distracted and unhappy employees, it is surely smarter to put out some commonsense guidelines that will help them, and their co-workers, cope with their relationships.

I have always believed that a good company should behave like an extended family and, as anyone who has ever raised children knows, dealing with such slings and arrows is simply part of family life.

EARN YOUR CUSTOMERS' TRUST

And their loyalty will follow

Q: I recently became my own boss, joining forces with my brother, who has an established operation. I am enjoying this experience, but finding ways to draw attention to our business and earning customers' trust is extremely tough.

Drawing a distinction between a businessman and an entrepreneur, if you had to choose one thing that defined your success what would it be?

– Randall De Freitas, Trinidad & Tobago

A: *Congratulations on your new venture! Working for yourself and your family can be a rewarding experience.*

At the same time, setting up a new business is tough, and most fail within the first year – usually thanks to a poorly executed plan, a lack of public awareness and/or a shortage of money. At the beginning of my career, I always tried to address the first two problems by ensuring that we had a great product or service and that everyone knew about our businesses because of our great publicity and cheeky advertising.

I believed that if we addressed those two critical issues, it would be easier to tackle the third challenge: generating enough cash to keep the business going. On the whole this method worked, and, as Virgin expanded, we set up new ventures when we felt we had a great business plan and could successfully challenge lazy market leaders in a sector that was ready for shaking up.

In assessing where Virgin has not got it right, a clear pattern emerges: our businesses didn't succeed when the Virgin difference was much harder for customers to grasp – when we launched products such as drinks, cosmetics and clothing. These Virgin businesses had limited marketing budgets and distribution channels compared to their well-established rivals and, because of the differentiation problem, found it difficult to create lasting awareness of and interest in their products.

By nature, I am anything but a numbers man, so I did not measure the success of a new venture by the amount of money we made. In Virgin Music's early days, we wanted to create great places to listen to music and meet friends. My sense was that if our staff liked our stores, there was a good chance our customers would too. At

Virgin Records, we had a similar attitude. On principle, we would only take on bands and artists that we thought were fun to work with – which meant we signed acts like the Sex Pistols and the Rolling Stones. Then we would create a stir about them.

This brings me to a secret to lasting success: securing your customers' trust, which should be part and parcel of your differentiation and marketing. At Virgin, we first did this somewhat accidentally, by relying on openness and simplicity when we communicated with our customers. Since we'd created companies everyone on staff was proud of, we were all deeply concerned about quality and customer service, and our marketing focused on why the businesses were different and special.

Tying my name to the Virgin brand also helped to foster a sense of brand accountability. When I was preparing to launch Virgin Atlantic Airways, Sir Freddie Laker gave me a key bit of advice about the importance of getting noticed. He said that as Virgin did not have the budget to compete with mainstream brands, the clever use of challenges – such as our attempts at setting world records by boat and balloon – would help to raise the airline's profile.

The strategy worked. We often made the headlines while spending a fraction of what our rivals did on marketing. This also meant that we put a face to our brand early on. I also encouraged customers to email me directly and advised our CEOs to do the same, which strengthened our ties with the customers.

Over time, this seems to have protected us from taking on many of the bad habits of large companies. Our emphasis on service, keeping a good sense of humour and on making sure our employees 'own' the businesses has helped us to build relationships with our customers. Over the years, we have won their trust, and their confidence gives us added impetus to give back in return.

Many of our advertising campaigns play off this open, frank communication. Our mobile phone companies offer straightforward bills with no hidden charges; our credit card agreements are easy to understand; our health club members are not locked into lengthy contracts.

In the current business environment, it may be tough not to focus solely on the numbers, but I believe this strategy of differentiating and marketing your product with a view to winning customers' trust is the only way to build a sustainable, lasting business. If times get tough, do not lose heart. You have already identified your key challenges, so just keep your message simple, direct, honest – and very public.

If you do, you and your brother should go far.

TO WORK BETTER
Holiday better

In July, as I'm writing this, many people, especially in the northern hemisphere, are already on holiday or about to go. It's a time of year when business people may find it especially tough to turn off their BlackBerrys and otherwise maintain work–life balance. It is indeed difficult: these days, business is global and fast-paced, and you may be emailed, texted or called at just about any time 24/7 by colleagues and clients, which means that you are expected always to keep an eye on the latest developments at your company. In this environment, decisions are often made too quickly by people who are too tired to make the best choices – a situation that over time will stunt a business's growth and its chances of success.

When I meet with groups of colleagues or business people, I sometimes ask how they would arrange their work hours differently if given the chance. Would they like to share a job, take more time off or work more flexibly?

Most people are reluctant to speak up, no matter what the situation, because they worry that their bosses will think they are lazy or lack motivation. Though many people are eager to change their work schedule, only about one in five executives immediately volunteers that information. If I persist in my questions, it usually turns out that more than half of the group wishes that their company would be more flexible about the structure of the work day.

It is important to tackle this problem, whether you are launching a business or managing an established one, because keeping your staff motivated and happy is key to the company's success. My experience and that of our group over the years has shown that making yourself take a break and ensuring that your employees or colleagues are able to do the same – and, better still, pursue their own outside interests – will help you to retain your most valuable team members. They will also be more creative and innovative, delivering better results overall.

Try asking your key people how best you can help them pursue their goals at work and at home. Maybe it could mean changing the structure of the work week or even something as radical as making non-emergency weekend messaging taboo. You can bet their spouses will like that one!

Some may be candidates for job sharing, an alternative that will help you to retain skilled older workers and others who cannot work full time – new parents, for example, or those caring for ill or elderly family members. This solution may create jobs since there are many people working full time who would voluntarily decrease their hours if given the chance, and many qualified unemployed people who would take part-time jobs if they were available.

Senior managers in particular may have difficulty accepting their colleagues' entering job-sharing arrangements for fear that those executives may lose touch with developments in their areas and miss something important. But there are few jobs that cannot be shared between two or more people. In fact, these fears reflect the reality that many executives are overburdened; that companies often assign too much responsibility to a single position. By introducing job sharing – and, frankly, better delegating the workload – companies can ensure that knowledge and experience are more widespread, and that decisions are made by those who are best positioned to do so. The saying 'two heads are better than one' can also be observed playing itself out in real life!

It's also important to take a good look at your company's policies regarding national holidays and paid holiday leave. Sadly, in some countries, particularly the United States, companies do not allow employees enough time to relax and recharge. There, the traditional base vacation allowance of just ten days is downright measly and just not enough; this attitude of discouraging employees from taking vacations only serves to encourage absenteeism and unhappiness. In Europe, most businesses have a better sense of what is appropriate and what will work for both employee and employer.

Remember, your generosity will pay off! There is always room to accommodate your employees' needs. If money is tight because you're running a start-up or your business is in the early stages, you can offer more time off in return for lower wages. In bigger, more established companies, long-serving employees should be offered the option of taking a sabbatical or unpaid leave – whatever is needed to recharge their batteries. And not just once every twenty years!

Finally, once you have established a trusted team, don't be afraid to let people work from home now and then. Many find they are more productive as they no longer have to commute and can use the quiet of their home office to focus on a project. I am fortunate that I can swim around Necker Island almost every morning; by cutting your journey to work, you could use the time to go to the gym or just spoil yourself with a cappuccino and read the paper for fifteen minutes at your favourite coffee shop.

Urging your people (and yourself) to take regular holidays and make time for family and other interests may seem counterintuitive in this fast-moving world, but try to think of it as an exercise in corporate security. By maintaining the health and mental wellbeing of your staff you are simply protecting the company's greatest asset – your people. If you map out their needs and find solutions, you'll see a huge payoff in terms of their creativity, energy, enthusiasm and teamwork – and, ultimately, in the success of your business.

Now get up from behind that desk and go for a walk. Talk to a few colleagues and ask 'If you could be doing something else right now what would it be?' The answers might surprise you.

STRIKE UP
THE BRAND
Living the values

A lot of people ask me about the Virgin brand – what's our secret? What's the enduring magic formula?

The truth is, we started with a really simple idea that has developed over time. When I opened my first record store, I thought it might be a success if I made it a cool place to hang out and kept prices low. I hoped that the combination would make the store popular and that the resulting sales volume would make up for lower prices. Although I didn't know it at the time, these basic notions were the beginning of what's now called brand values. At Virgin, ours include providing good value for money and a great customer experience.

I firmly believed back then, and still do now, that you can apply those rudimentary values to any business situation. Today Virgin has become one of the most diverse brands in the world as we have continued breaking into new markets and shaking them up for the customer's benefit. And our brand values are the glue that holds it all together.

That doesn't mean our business is a complete free-for-all, as my team often reminds me. Though we receive proposals for almost every imaginable product and service – drinks, plastic surgery, clothing, restaurants, care for the elderly, even funeral services – we have a central team that evaluates each idea to see if it fits with our values and what consumers expect of Virgin. Sometimes the debate is fierce!

And then sometimes our risk-taking pays dividends, such as our turnaround of Britain's NTL:Telewest cable business, which became the successful, customer-focused business now known as Virgin Media. This major effort involved moving some of our best people into that business and changing the focus from quarterly sales targets to longer-term goals that involved keeping customers happy and loyal. Keeping customers and employees happy is good for the business, and not a cost that can be cut!

As nice as it is to read articles that say the Virgin brand is one of the most powerful in the world, our corporate goal is to make it one of the most trusted.

To this end we have put together a structure to ensure that every company in the Virgin Group is fully attuned to our values as well as the customer expectations that accompany them. We provide brand training for all our businesses and supply the tools they need. We set targets at all our call centres for customer satisfaction and measure them on a regular basis. We bring together all our marketing departments to share ideas. And every new business gets all this help right from the start.

We try to lay out how we will make Virgin even stronger in the future. Regardless of how respected Virgin has become – we now operate in over thirty countries, employ over 50,000 people and serve millions of customers every month – we cannot be complacent. We focus on core areas that all Virgin companies must treat as priorities in order for the brand to flourish. These include everything from Virgin brand basics to connecting with customers online. It also emphasises collaboration among Virgin companies, entrepreneurialism, ethics – and also music, fun and rock 'n' roll! In essence, it is a route map connecting our past to our future.

I often mention people – not sales statistics or the bottom line – because, as I hope I have made very clear in this book, I truly believe that our people are the heart and soul of our brand. The simple concept of offering customers a better experience, and having fun while you do it, attracts very bright and enthusiastic people. That said, as important as it is to have gifted, creative types developing great products and marketing, it will all go for naught if the people at the sharp end aren't delivering it to our customers, in the right way, 24/7. This emphasis on the importance of every one of our people is what really makes Virgin's brand values something more than a dusty mission statement stuffed into a drawer somewhere.

In business schools, brand values are often discussed in terms of marketing, as though they are an end result of a scientific process, rather than embedded in a business's soul. Thankfully, I've learned that in the real world of business it's better to rely on creativity, intuition and empathy. You can hire consultants to build a brand using a hands-off, theoretical approach, but you'll do far better – and have more fun – if, like Virgin did, you nurture your own.

SHARING LIFE'S LESSONS

Mentors can make it happen

Can entrepreneurship be taught? Can an aspiring business leader learn to choose the right plan, take the right risks, select the right team and then navigate all the turbulence that follows?

With most of the West's major economies showing sluggish growth at best, many in politics and business are keen to find answers, because a new wave of energetic entrepreneurs is urgently needed to kick-start trade all over the world, shake up the markets and create jobs.

In my experience, success as an entrepreneur depends upon a fairly unusual combination of personality traits and instinctive skills, most of which can only be honed on the job. Formal coursework may be a start but is certainly not enough. Most entry-level entrepreneurs need the kind of guidance that only a trusted mentor can provide.

It's critical that experienced executives and CEOs

volunteer to coach young entrepreneurs in their communities: this is one of the most immediately rewarding and concrete ways successful business leaders can foster economic growth in their region. There are many young entrepreneurs who, if they are given the critical boost of great advice as they launch their start-ups, will someday bring in new jobs. To find a mentoring group in your area, consult local universities, industry groups and small-business development centres.

As I mentioned earlier our team has set up two Branson Centres of Entrepreneurship, non-profit organisations where entrepreneurs, mentors, community members and investors can gather to discuss projects, learn practical skills and spread the word about their ideas.

Since we set up the first Branson Centre in Johannesburg six years ago, more than a hundred entrepreneurs have taken part in our programme, and, at present, eleven of their businesses are in operation, employing many people. One of our more recent 'graduates' is Lesego Malatsi, a fashion designer and entrepreneur whose stunning designs were showcased at London Fashion Week in September 2011.

We opened the second school in Jamaica in late 2011 and a new class of fifteen people is working on launching businesses in everything from hospitality to education services to recycling.

Do you know someone trying to start a business? As a mentor, there are six things you should keep in mind:

I. A good coach tells it straight

Don't sugarcoat it! Your most important job is to help a beginning entrepreneur cut through confusion and misinformation to the truth. The evaluations may be intensely personal: what sort of leadership style do they have? What can they do to improve? It may be difficult for your mentee to hear your critical comments, but you must explain very clearly what is going wrong.

2. Build a mentoring team

Many entrepreneurs need help in more than one area. When I started out, my dyslexia made keeping accounts difficult so a family friend who was an accountant stepped in and helped me. His advice was crucial in helping me to understand how things worked and how to run a business. If you are unable to provide all the advice your mentee needs, help them find someone who can.

3. Teach them to be bold

When the founders of our centre in Jamaica evaluated prospective students for the current class, they found that all of those who applied identified obtaining better access to capital through our programme as a key goal, but only 14 per cent had asked for a loan. In different cultures, there are different barriers to approaching prospective investors; almost everyone needs advice and help in this area. Share your experiences, review the pitches and practise approaches.

4. Make the introductions

Start-ups often struggle to attract customers and then to keep costs under control as orders increase. Access to investors makes all the difference for many businesses. Be prepared to call industry contacts and old friends; whatever it takes to help your mentees connect with those who will see the potential in their projects.

5. Get the message out

When I was first getting into the airline business, Sir Freddie Laker advised me to build company promotions around my own personality — a strategy that has worked well for Virgin. Freddie believed that small entrepreneurial businesses could survive and prosper if they were known about and marketed properly. Potential marketing opportunities are often overlooked by newcomers — help them by pointing out the possibilities.

6. Persistence is key

Setting up a business is a risky occupation. It is important that we help newcomers understand that an early venture's failure is a badge of experience, not the end of one's career; that the most important thing to do if things go wrong is to learn from it and bounce back.

So go to it! Make it happen and not just be something you 'always mentor do' — sorry!

POWER TO THE PEOPLE

Turning the pyramid upside down

Q: Some business leaders believe that the customer should always come first, many will always put shareholders first, while others argue that employees should come first. So who *should* come first: shareholders, employees or customers?

– Eden Kironde, Uganda

A: *Conventional wisdom holds that companies should see to their shareholders' needs first, their customers' second and their employees' last of all. We have always turned this pyramid on its head; at all the Virgin Group companies our employees come first, then our customers, then our shareholders. It's simply common sense: if your workforce is happy and well-motivated, your customers are more likely to be happy as well – which means there's a greater chance that your business will see strong sales and good* *profits, generating the results that your shareholders demand.*

We stumbled on this formula when we were launching our record-store business in the late sixties. We decided to look for employees who were passionate about music, because we thought their enthusiasm and knowledge would be as important a draw as the beanbags, free coffee and listening posts we planned to feature in our first stores – and that turned out to be correct. Our employees were able to help music aficionados find new bands, and to assist customers new to the music scene to develop and expand their tastes.

When we launched Virgin Records a couple of years later, it naturally followed that the staff should be as passionate as those at our other businesses. We put a lot of effort into finding and hiring the right people, and then we made sure that they felt empowered to run the business as they saw fit – that's what we had employed them for. This approach helped us to attract and keep great talent. Those employees found and signed the artists that soon made Virgin Records the world's largest independent label, attracting a generation of fans.

It can be difficult to ensure that this focus on employees continues across an organistion, especially as your business grows and diversifies, but it is certainly well worth the effort. Virgin has launched four hundred businesses in more than forty years of expansion; our focus on our employees is one of the main reasons for our success. We maintained a common culture that unites our businesses and ensures that we retain a strong, loyal following among our customers. You can see it in every employee's can-do, blunt, if slightly irreverent attitude. One small way we try to keep this culture alive and thriving, is to throw a number of our employees together as a team to work on a project. We ask them to apply from all over the world to join a week long volunteer trip to a community outside our game reserve in Ulusaba. Working with colleagues from other Virgin companies brings to life all the Virgin values.

If you decide to take your business down this path, you'll need to find great business leaders who are also outstanding communicators, or develop these skills yourself. As CEO, you must be able to gauge the mood of your workforce. Are your employees interested and creative, or are some of them uncommunicative or withdrawn? If you sense a problem, you must uncover any underlying rivalries or resentments and defuse tensions quickly, before they impact morale. In the service industry, it is crucial to get this right, as nothing will ever mask a staff member's surliness.

Do your employees or colleagues feel that their voices count? If an employee spots a problem, do they have the tools to fix it? If another has a good idea, is there a venue for sharing it? This is the other aspect of communication that you must master: making sure that front-line employees are able to contact you, so that you and your team can act on their information.

When a CEO has created clear channels of communication throughout his company, front-line employees are more likely to feel positive, empowered and able to make a difference. Customers will know the difference – and love it.

In 1997, when we took over the West Coast Main Line, we also took over management of its crumbling infrastructure, its ageing fleet of trains and its demotivated, long-suffering workforce. On the day we relaunched the rail service, the passengers saw almost no difference, except for a splash of Virgin red paint. Today, we are the most popular network in the UK, with a passenger approval rating of more than 90 per cent, and our trains carry more than twice as many passengers. We have won market share from the airlines and have changed the public's perception of train travel.

Some of the expansion can be attributed to 'stuff' like track upgrades and our new fleet of high-speed trains, but at the core of our success is the job that was done by chief executive Tony Collins and his team. He chose only people who reflected his own passion, energy and imagination, and who worked tirelessly to relay our vision to the staff and instil a strong sense of Virgin's culture and pride – it wasn't an overnight turnaround but what we have today is as night and day to what we inherited. An effective CEO is a leader, a mentor and a manager, and at the same time must be deeply involved in the day-to-day workings of the business. His or her responsibilities are to all the interested *parties, but if the first priority remains the employees, all the other people (like shareholders and customers) can only come out as winners.*

Some businesses will view 50,000 employees as nothing more than a cost to be managed, but at Virgin I see 50,000 passionate brand ambassadors.

WATCHING YOUR WAISTLINE

Will help the bottom line

Being your own boss and travelling the world can seem like a very glamorous lifestyle, and in many ways it is, but take it from one who knows – it can also be very tough on body and mind.

Being an entrepreneur is hard work – the long hours, the stress – and unless you take steps to regain a work–life balance it can eventually take a toll on your health. For an entrepreneur or chief executive leading a growing company, keeping fit and taking breaks from work is not a nicety, it's a necessity: you have to plan for personal health and fitness in the same way you plan for profits and growth. This will help you to keep a fresh perspective on any problems your company encounters and, ultimately, to make better business decisions.

As I write I have just returned from an exhausting tour in which I visited five continents in less than a month. It started with a memorable week in New Zealand, then on to Chile, Brazil, South Africa and the UK before finishing up in India. I have always travelled extensively, ever since we founded Virgin. At first, I was helping to build Virgin Records into a global music business; now, with our new business development focused on emerging markets and many of our Virgin Unite philanthropic initiatives based in Africa and Asia, it is unlikely that I will be able to slow the pace and extent of my travel. Staying alert and being effective on such gruelling trips takes preparation and lots of self-discipline.

Luckily for me, fitness has always been a hobby. At school I was a keen sportsman until a knee injury cut short my hopes of professional success. Unable to pursue my sporting dreams, I threw myself into my early business career and set up *Student* magazine. My passion for sport remained, and I have continued to play tennis, swim, ski (on snow and water), sail and, more recently, to kite surf.

I try to fit in at least one good workout per day, and sometimes two, if I have the opportunity. Our home on Necker Island is a great place for me to keep up my swimming. Most mornings when I am there, I head off for a swim around the island – about three miles. It is the best way to clear the head (sometimes from the excesses of the night before!) and sets one up for the day.

Set on its own at the end of the archipelago of islands, Necker is also a great place to sail and kite surf. After a long day of correspondence or calls, there is nothing better than setting off on my kite board – I soon feel invigorated and renewed.

Fitness goals aside, it is important to do something that helps you to achieve distance from the pressures of work. Many people who are faced with the increasing pressures of the modern, global and 'always-on' business world struggle to stop working. By focusing on something else – in my case, on sport – you gain perspective on other areas of your life, and this helps you to achieve that elusive work–life balance.

Many of my pastimes are ones that my family enjoys, too, which has helped a great deal. There is no better way to forget the stresses of a poorly performing company or the frustrations of not closing a deal than kite surfing with your kids or going snow skiing with them.

During periods of travel, you have to plan for your exercise. In April 2010, when I signed up for the London Marathon to coincide with Virgin Money's sponsoring the race, I faced the challenge of trying to fit the intensive training regimen into an already busy speaking and travel programme. Together with a coach, I mapped out the training runs I needed to do and looked at my destinations to try to make them match up. It was great fun. As I circled the world, I found myself running in the parks of Sydney, along the beach in Barcelona, and through the bush at our Ulusaba Private Game Reserve in South Africa.

Luckily, my children Holly and Sam had also decided to run the race with a group of friends, so we often trained together on our family breaks. This helped to maintain some friendly family competition and ensured that we all remained focused on the challenge ahead. On race day, we all completed the race in good time and, along with their thirty-two team-mates,

Holly and Sam set a world record for the most people (thirty-four no less!) to finish a marathon while tied together.

Occasionally things don't go according to plan. That same year, all three of us tried to kite surf across the English Channel, but rough seas quickly foiled our attempt. In January, a skiing accident caused me to snap my anterior cruciate ligament (ACL) and so I was unable to run, ski or kite surf for more than six months. As a way of motivating myself to keep fit during that period, I threw myself into training for the swimming leg of the London Triathlon. Holly and Sam completed all three legs of the race, so we all had a great time.

At Virgin, I am notorious for constantly inventing challenges that will help us to push ourselves harder – and that includes physically. But making small changes can be even more helpful in the long run. Next time you settle down on a Sunday morning to answer that mountain of email, think about whether you might be better off first going for a brisk walk, run, swim or bike ride to refresh the body and the mind.

Remember, very few people have ever lain on their deathbed and thought, 'You know, I really wish I had spent more time in the office.'

WHAT'S BETTER THAN A HANDOUT?

A hand up

The recent surge in natural disasters all over the world serves as a sombre reminder to us of the fragile hold we have on the planet. The shortest tremor can cause untold damage. When it happens in a location like Haiti, hundreds of thousands can die and the lives of millions are affected.

The world will usually respond by sending rescue team, tents, food, clean water and medicine. Governments, companies, celebrities, everyday individuals, churches and school groups will jump in to assist with donations, fundraising events and all nature of spontaneous aid.

In the midst of this tremendous reaction, one of the biggest tasks is always the coordination of the resources and funding to make sure they get to the front lines in an effective and timely manner.

The challenges Haiti faced in the months following the horrendous earthquake there in early 2010 reminds us of the need for a strong combination of governments, corporations, non-governmental organisations and individuals working together. It is an effective and powerful mix, so long as it is controlled by informed people on the front lines. Something that sadly is not always the case!

While the world recession of the last several years has put a crimp in the funding many in the non-profit sector rely upon, it has also prompted the latest generation of philanthropists to look at ways of working together more effectively to ensure that the best initiatives do the most good on as large a scale as possible.

For example, Jeff Skoll, one of the founders of eBay, used his entrepreneurial skills to establish Participant, a new film company that focuses on combining entertainment with building awareness of major world issues. His films range from *An Inconvenient Truth*, the great documentary about climate change, and *The Soloist*, a beautiful film highlighting the issue of homelessness in the United States, to *Countdown to Zero*, a film about the need to rid the world of nuclear weapons.

Individual fortunes larger than the gross domestic product of many countries have been created in the past twenty years. In response, we need a more benevolent form of capitalism, one that creates wealth and also then spends some of that wealth more responsibly. Business has a new sense of purpose: to prove that capitalism on its own is not enough. We must turn a profit while making the world a better place.

For some people this has involved creating large foundations to distribute wealth; for others, it has meant putting social responsibility and good business practices at the heart of their organisations.

Occasionally it has spelled the demise of the 'golden charity cheque' and the birth of new, aid-free, entrepreneurial approaches to giving. The debate continues about whether pure charity is better than giving that fosters economic growth – but the debate is futile. The world needs all the help it can get right now to tackle the scale of the environmental and social problems we are facing.

A few years ago we created the not-for-profit foundation Virgin Unite for our businesses and partners. It is quite simply about connecting people who can tackle tough challenges using entrepreneurial approaches. We want to be catalysts for new ways to deal with providing health care on a large scale, encouraging peace and diminishing factors that contribute to climate change.

As I mentioned earlier, we established the Elders, a group of wise men and women including Nelson Mandela, Archbishop Desmond Tutu, Jimmy Carter, Kofi Annan and Mary Robinson, to name a few, who work quietly behind the scenes, seeking to resolve global conflicts.

We are working to set up a Disease Control Hub in partnership with the South African government and health leaders to help eradicate suffering from preventable and treatable diseases.

Since we don't pretend to have all the answers, we work with great partners and experts to make sure we are always informed by the people who are in the thick of the issues.

Often, almost by default, these people at the sharp end may know the answers but have just not had the chance for their voices to be heard.

It is exciting to see different sectors of civic life forge new and even unlikely partnerships to tackle big challenges. Coupled with technology that truly interconnects the world, our initiatives can succeed on a larger scale than ever before. As globalisation increases the divide between the rich and the poor, we must harness technology and entrepreneurial skills to build a more prosperous and healthy world for everyone.

That requires us – with a great sense of humility and respect – to engage with partners and people on the front lines. We always get as much as we give. Solutions can come at a low cost if we keep this generation of philanthropists engaged and involved.

HOME AND/OR OFFICE
Finding the balance

Perhaps it's the fact that I've always managed to organise my life so as to be able to work from home that leads to the frequent question, 'Richard, how do you think people like me should balance the demands of work and family?' For many an aspiring entrepreneur and business person struggling with the dual responsibilities of a career and a family can really be a major issue.

Here are just three variations on this important question that have come up repeatedly over the years.

Can you be a successful entrepreneur and still devote time to your family?

You can and *must* make time for both family and business. It is important to build a strong family life which also helps to give you a better perspective and balance in business. Moreover, a key responsibility for each generation is to bring up the next one – and you need to be present to do this.

Having almost always worked from home, it's been relatively easy for me to spend time with my family. Once, my 'office' was a small houseboat in Little Venice, and I fondly remember the kids crawling around the floor while I had my meetings. I particularly recall the look of horror on my bank manager's face when a runny-nosed child rubbed up against his pin-striped suit!

Even when we moved to a 'proper' house in Holland Park, I used it as an office and moved out only when my wife, Joan, complained about people lining up in the hallway for meetings in our home. Mind you, I relocated the office all of two doors down the road!

How do you balance family life with the time required to set up and build a business?

Spending a lot of time with the family also made me adapt the way I work. This has been one of the keys to Virgin's success. To offset working from home I always made sure we had proper family holidays – time spent away from the home/office. Spending time away taught me the importance of delegating. I quickly learned what I was good at and made sure I brought in people to help with those areas where I was weaker.

As Virgin got bigger and we set up more businesses, they had to be run from actual offices in various buildings. I minimised the time I spent inside those buildings. This helped me keep the bigger picture in perspective, remaining alert to new opportunities. I could focus on the important decisions without getting bogged down with too many daily details. Taking yourself outside the hurly-burly of everyday business allows you to make clearer and longer-term decisions.

Being away from the office for periods of time also means you develop a strong bond of trust with your senior colleagues. In my case, we have built a very strong team of committed and talented managers who will fight for the business through the tough times.

There is a balance, though, and you must be careful not to be too distant or absent from a company. An entrepreneur must be highly visible and readily available to the staff and spend time getting their feedback and ideas. Listening to others is a key quality of a good business leader.

How important to you is it to take time off?

A lack of sufficient time off and short holidays are constant bugbears in the modern business world. To keep yourself and your staff motivated and healthy, it is important to take holidays and get a break from work. The right balance will ensure that you have a healthy, committed and enthusiastic staff who perform better when at work instead of looking for excuses to take sick days.

Keeping fit and healthy is also a key to staying on top in business. Exercising every day – a brisk walk, a swim, a run or a game of tennis – gives me more energy to tackle the everyday decisions. My philosophy of living life to the fullest and taking advantage of good family holidays has also turned up a few business opportunities along the way. On a trip to

Africa we discovered Ulusaba, our stunning game reserve near the Kruger National Park. While in Morocco, waiting for the balloon expedition to take off, my family discovered the Kasbah Tamadot, nestled in the Atlas Mountains. Both of these properties are now key parts of the Virgin Limited Edition portfolio.

Actually, many of my business opportunities have come through personal experiences on my travels – during the time that is really blurred between work and play. I may have met someone who triggered an idea or visited a place that sparked a new venture.

As I've already discussed, it is really important that companies are more flexible in how they approach staff and time off – through job sharing, flexible hours or working from home. Finding the right balance for yourself and your staff may be the key building block for a successful, resilient and happy business.

Now put this book down and go and play with your kids or visit a friend!

KICK-START THE ECONOMY

Ten tips

Recent instability in global stock markets reflects the fragility of the economic recovery in the United States, Europe and elsewhere. Confidence is low, debt is high and, in some cases, taxes are rising. While the market for goods and services is booming in the so-called 'BRIC' countries – Brazil, Russia, India and China – something needs to be done to restore the confidence that will spur demand around the world. We need a quick economic boost.

This is a key moment for the world's entrepreneurs, a fraternity that invariably seems to shoulder much of the burden in restarting stalled economies. Governments also need to answer the call as they alone can tackle the really big-ticket projects.

Here are my top ten tips for what I think needs to be done – and who needs to do it.

1. Show us the money

Make sure banks lend the money they're sitting on, at attractive terms, to small and medium-sized businesses. Pumping money into new products and services is the best way to deliver more jobs and growth. Who has to do it? Politicians. They bailed out the banks; they need to make sure the banks don't lock up the keys to recovery.

2. Look overseas for investors

Foreign direct investment is a tonic for the weak sectors of any economy but antiquated citizenship regulations should not be allowed to prohibit it where there is no possible threat to national security. Every country needs to revisit its tax incentives – especially those nations in decline. Large multinationals want a skilled workforce and stable political environment; given that, investment, manufacturing and jobs will follow.

3. Improve the infrastructure

When the financial crisis broke in 2008, Barack Obama suggested focusing on relatively small 'shovel-ready' infrastructure projects, to supply jobs and kick-start the economy. Fine, but the US also needs to roll out more and bigger projects, and governments around the world should do likewise: motorways and railways to connect cities, increased capacity on railway lines and roads, better airports, new bridges; safe, updated infrastructure works. It will allow companies to move to areas best suited to their needs.

4. Keep it simple

Reducing the red tape involved in hiring new employees and setting up businesses is a no-brainer. Why does the process remain lengthy and expensive almost everywhere?

5. Zoom past fossil fuels

The cost of fuel is rising and supplies of oil and natural gas are uncertain in an increasingly unstable world. Investing in renewable energy will create opportunities for skilled workers, lower costs across the board and assure an energy supply for the next generation. The public and private sectors must work together on this.

6. Adopt 'talent without borders'

Skilled and enterprising workers are needed in almost every market and sector. Yet employers must often jump through endless bureaucratic hoops to take advantage of the expertise available in the global marketplace. The world is flat now; its workforce is increasingly mobile. Have you set out the welcome mat?

7. Teach people to make things

Germany remains the European Union's powerhouse because of its very strong manufacturing and engineering capabilities. What's stopping other countries from borrowing the German model? The US has succeeded in technological innovation, but software and hardware design is increasingly shifting to new Silicon Valleys in India, China and, before long, Brazil. As odd as it may sound in this techno-world, manufacturing is now the new 'new frontier'. We can't take it for granted any more.

8. Abandon student 'warehouses'

In many fields (except maybe medicine) the duration of university degree courses could and should be shortened, enabling skilled people to move into the workplace more quickly, and, in countries like the US, with a less crippling student-loan burden. Colleges have become warehouses, storing students for as long as possible instead of preparing them effectively and efficiently for productive work.

9. Offer flexitime as well as full-time

Millions of workers around the world would prefer shorter hours but lack the option. Widespread adoption of job sharing and flexitime would dramatically reduce unemployment and its associated costs. People who wish to work less – often to spend more time with their families – would be able to do so, and some others would return to the workplace as a result. A win-win. Nothing but tradition is standing in the way.

10. Restore stability

Finally, a plea to leaders around the world: governments must lead the way to a stable financial environment. Interest rates should be set low; money must flow through the banking system. Controls on private enterprise are less important now than encouraging investment. Only this will give rise to the virtuous circle of new companies, new jobs and new markets that in turn will restore confidence and pride in our economies.

That's it – so let's get to it!

RULES OF THE ROAD

Everyone needs to know where they're going

Coaching senior managers can be difficult, simply because they need to find a stretch of uninterrupted time to review their decisions. So, every year, we bring senior managers from across the Virgin Group to my home on Necker Island to discuss the challenges and opportunities we face. We celebrate our achievements, reflect on our mistakes and discuss how we could better work together.

In a session led by Sally Morgan, a former aide to Tony Blair who now serves as one of our advisers, our group came up with some handy guidelines for managers by looking at lessons learned from the public, private and non-profit sectors. Whether you are launching your first start-up or leading an experienced team, these basics will hold true in almost every situation.

l. What's the plan? Keep your team informed

It is crucial to set objectives for each period according to your business's strategic direction – and then make sure that all employees know about them.

Sally told us that when she was working for the British government, every summer the ministers appointed to the Cabinet would receive a note from Tony Blair that outlined his overall strategic approach for the year and set clear objectives for each department.

The Cabinet would meet for a week to discuss these plans before Members of Parliament returned from their summer holidays and had the opportunity to analyse and challenge the approach. Thereafter, the team received a note from Blair every Sunday, which they would discuss at a meeting the next morning to agree on key actions.

Communicating your objectives regularly will help you to ensure that your team has a framework for making their own decisions. It is important that all must feel welcome to discuss the group's objectives – that open debate is encouraged – because everyone will have a collective responsibility to follow through.

2. Define the rules of the road

It is important to define a core set of values for your business, to which you and your employees can refer when making decisions.

When assessing investments and new directions at Virgin, we have always considered whether the proposed business meets our core values, which helps us to manage our diverse portfolio and maintain some consistency.

We look at whether the business will do something differently than most or all of the other companies in the industry or sector; whether it will provide real value, great customer service and still retain the sense of fun and pride that distinguishes a good business from a great business. More recently we have added a new core value: we also test whether a new business will have the legs to go overseas and can be scaled up within about three years.

3. Focus, focus, focus

It is always tempting to try to do too much; for ambitious managers and their teams, there always seem to be too many projects and too little time. But successful organisations know what their priorities are: they tackle the really important projects and the rest falls into place. Look at your strategic plan and rules of the road, and choose accordingly.

4. Who's in charge? It's up to you

A good manager provides clear roles for the members of their team, which enables everyone to get on with the job of running the business. Once you've made these choices, do not micromanage. If you make a habit of diving in and changing a major project's direction or otherwise intervening, your people will learn to be dependent on you, and they will never reach their full potential.

5. Champion your people's ideas

When your team makes a judgement call, you need to follow through with conviction. If you merely cast doubt and let their project languish, your team will not have the impetus or confidence to take the next steps. If you insist on making every big decision yourself, you will create a terrible logjam.

Don't fall into the trap of asking for endless reports in order to justify moving forward. It is always better to act; it is debilitating to dither.

6. When mistakes happen, learn from them and move on

It is impossible to get every decision right. When things go wrong, take time to review what happened with your team and learn from it together. But don't linger too long – just dust yourself off and tackle the next challenge.

7. Celebrate your successes

When someone on your team has a big success, celebrate it and tell others. Success breeds success. And this is something that should be a part of your everyday work – as I've said before, you should try to catch your team doing something right.

In short, if the best real estate is all about 'location, location, location', then the mantra for running the best business has got to be 'communication, communication, communication'.

SCHOOL OF HARD KNOCKS

Education starts at school but goes on forever

Q: You quit school at the age of sixteen, but went on to great success. Do you think a university diploma is necessary to become a successful person? I am a university student and sometimes I wonder whether I would do better without it. What are your thoughts?

I believe I have some great and even innovative ideas for new businesses, but face the difficulty of turning an idea into something real. What advice would you give me to overcome this step?

– Felipe Herriges, Brazil

A: There are lots of things in life we think we 'can't get enough of' and education is top of that list. I am fortunate that, at this stage of my career, I have the opportunity to learn about many new subjects, ranging from the impact of

climate change to way-out-there stuff like the possibility
of colonising Mars.

I am also lucky in that I meet so many interesting
people and have the opportunity to exchange ideas
with them – everyone from former leaders such as Kofi
Annan, Nelson Mandela and Mary Robinson to scientist
and environmentalist James Lovelock to Burt Rutan, the
engineer leading our Virgin Galactic project.

Indeed, since Virgin's projects and industries are so
varied and our foundation, Virgin Unite, challenges us to
try to solve some of our generation's biggest problems, my
companies provide me with an experience I often compare
to an extended university course. As a kid I never really
enjoyed going to school but I'm loving every minute of this
extraordinary journey.

But it was very different when I was young. School
wasn't easy. I was not a good student, partly because of
my dyslexia (which was not diagnosed until later) and
partly because of my restless nature. I found it hard to
concentrate in class and spent much of my time in school
dreaming up and setting up new mini-businesses.

The first few ventures I created – including one focused
on growing Christmas trees – did not succeed, but those
experiences did give me a taste for business and a
knowledge of the all-important art of delegation.

By the time I was sixteen I was ready to leave school,
but my father was reluctant to approve my decision. One
weekend he came to visit my boarding school and tried to

persuade me to continue my studies. He hoped I'd become a lawyer like him. I reluctantly agreed; he drove home to explain 'our' decision to my mother, Eve.

She was not happy! She told him to make the long drive back immediately, to reassure me that it was okay to leave. He did, and I left school that summer. I never once looked back, first setting up Student *magazine and, a few years later, the Virgin record stores. My father often joked that his second return trip was the 'best drive of his life'.*

However, my story is a very personal one; my strategy will not work for everyone. Particularly in today's tough jobs market, a degree or other diploma can be critical as it shows that you have gained the skills and other building blocks required to start your career.

But obtaining that diploma is only a first step, and in no way guarantees success. You'll need a great work ethic and determination to make it – both in business and life. You also need your fair share of good luck.

I would advise tackling your studies with a positive attitude – try to enjoy your time at university. Try a few new things while you are there, and maybe even start a business, if this is where your interests lie.

We have set up the Branson Centre of Entrepreneurship to help foster budding entrepreneurs and their fledgling companies. Most of our students are young men and women, determined to study hard and build their businesses. One of the most important things we impart to them is the importance of enjoying your work.

When you reach the launch stage, don't be afraid to make that first leap.

Most entrepreneurs' first ventures fail – I know, because mine did – but the lessons you learn from failure are invaluable and will help you with your next attempts. You have to be very determined and accept that the early stages of launching any business are mostly about just surviving.

Turning an idea into reality is a key step that all entrepreneurs have to master. Try to see your ideas through your customers' eyes – it'll help you determine which ideas have a chance of succeeding. You should also check out the competitive forces that might work against you. When I was a boy, if I had looked at my ill-fated Christmas tree business through the eyes of a hungry rabbit I might have thought twice about sinking my savings into it!

Good luck, Felipe! Please hang in there and complete your education, throw everything into your studies and remember: whether you're working for a company or setting up your own business, work hard, persevere and smile, and you will be on the road to success.

ACKNOWLEDGEMENTS

As with everything else in my life, I am grateful to a lot of people for the inspiration behind, and the creation of, *Like a Virgin*. To name but a few ...

Thanks must go to Nick Fox at Virgin Management for constantly urging me to 'write it down' and then sometimes taking dictation from all over the world as I took him up on the advice; and to Gloria Anderson and Patti Sonntag at the *New York Times* for commissioning and then syndicating some of my scribblings to more than fifty countries.

Then there's David Tait, who built Virgin Atlantic in the USA from day one and has spent the best part of thirty years correcting my English. David was a great support in helping me order my thoughts and making these outpourings readable.

Not least, my thanks go out to two more important groups. All the readers of the various publications around the world and others who have texted, blogged or emailed (one even came in on a postcard) all nature of thought-provoking comments, opinions and questions, many of which I have attempted to respond to in these pages.

And, secondly, to all the wonderful employees past and present of the Virgin Group who have helped me create our unusual family of companies and have helped me fill this book with great stories and lessons.

I hope it spurs on a new generation of entrepreneurs.

Thank you one and all.

INDEX